My Inventions

Bust of Tesla by Ivan Meštrović.
(Tesla Museum/Smithsonian Institution)

MY INVENTIONS

The Autobiography of
NIKOLA TESLA

Edited, with an Introduction, by
Ben Johnston

hart brothers
AUSTIN, TEXAS

Acknowledgements

The editor wishes to thank Elliot Sivowitch of the Smithsonian Institution and Nicholas Kosanovich of the Tesla Memorial Society for help in obtaining photographs. A further debt is owed Al Ulmer, Robin Ulmer, and Geraldine Kochan for invaluable advice freely offered.

Professional photographic services deserving recognition were performed by the Library of Congress photoduplication staff, by photographer Fred Hill of Burlington, Vermont, and by Paul Patnaude of the Offset House, South Burlington. Michele Bottiggi (also of the Offset House) designed the book, Stephen Nelson prepared the map, and Geraldine Kochan provided the stipple portrait of Tesla that appears on the paperback cover.

Published by Hart Brothers
Post Office Box 5690, Austin, Texas 78763-5690

My Inventions originally appeared
in the *Electrical Experimenter* magazine in 1919.
First Hart Brothers edition October 1982
7   8   9   10

Library of Congress Catalog Card Number: 82-82495

ISBN 0-910077-01-0 Hardcover
ISBN 0-910077-00-2 Paperback

PRINTED IN THE UNITED STATES OF AMERICA

CONTENTS

Editor's note:

Parts I through V of
My Inventions
were published in the
Electrical Experimenter
monthly magazine from February through June of 1919,
with part VI following in October, 1919.

Tesla's idiosyncratic phonetic spellings have not been changed in this
edition. All of the original illustrations have been reproduced, and six new illustrations have been added. Several of the original picture captions have been altered to
improve accuracy or clarity. Only the promotional material with which the original editor introduced each of the six serial installments has been omitted altogether. This reflects the present editor's desire that Tesla's work be allowed to
stand on its own, as it is eminently capable of doing.

B.J.

INTRODUCTION

I

Nikola Tesla wrote the six magazine articles comprising *My Inventions* in 1919, when he was 63 years old and well past the peak of his career. He was still a public figure, however, and his fame was solidly rooted: at age 31, four years after his 1884 emigration from Europe to the United States, he had dramatically presented to the world his polyphase alternating current system — the electrical power system today employed worldwide.[1] (See p. 63 for a description.) Tesla's system made Edison's *direct* current system, itself inaugurated only in the early 1880's, almost obsolete by the turn of the century. These waning years of the 19th century were Tesla's most prolific period; the triumphant opening of the huge Niagara Falls polyphase hydroelectric plant in 1895 by itself would have secured his reputation, but he had long since moved into the dazzling field of "high frequency" mechanical and electrical vibrations. Tesla amazed his peers with mechanical oscillators which vibrated thousands of times a second and were capable of disintegrating steel; his electrical oscillators, unhindered by mechanical inertia, produced even more rapidly vibrating (or alternating) *currents* which seemed endowed with magical qualities. During the 1890's, these high frequency electrical currents became widely known as "Tesla currents."

The polyphase electric system revolutionized the way mankind used power soon after Tesla unveiled it in 1888, but the startling discovery of radio waves, announced by Heinrich Hertz in the same year, immediately overshadowed even the celebrated "battle" between Tesla's alternating and Edison's direct current systems. Hertz opened the door to wireless communication, yet before radio could become a reality, other equally stunning discoveries burst forth: electrons, x-rays, and radioactivity all entered the human vocabulary in rapid succession. The modern era of mind-boggling change, product of a spiraling world population and its ever-growing control of the lightning forces of electricity, had begun in earnest. Tesla's command of high frequency currents placed him at the forefront of late-nineteenth-century research into x-rays, diathermy, discharge lighting, robotics, and wireless — his lectures on these and other subjects were stunning successes. His work culminated with the 1899 demonstration in Chicago of an elaborate radio-controlled boat, followed in the same year by construction in Colorado of a giant experimental wireless transmitter.

Unfortunately, Tesla's unorthodox theories of wireless transmission (which he thought was more an air or earth current-conduction than a free space wave-propagation phenomenon) and his fixation on transmitting wireless *power* as well as messages prevented his pioneering wireless work from being formally recognized in the United States for many years. Only in 1943, (several months after his death) did the Supreme Court void Marconi's fundamental United States wireless patent because of prior work by Tesla, Oliver Lodge, and John Stone Stone[2]. The Court's belated reversal of quarter-century-old lower court opinions favoring Marconi's patent must rank as a landmark example of slamming the barn door after the horses had not only bolted but also died of old age: all of the patentees and patents involved in the suit had expired, and the plaintiff, the Marconi Wireless Telegraph Company of America, had long since been superseded by the American-owned Radio Corporation of America. (The defendant in the case was the United States Government, which had taken control of all United States wireless technology during World War I, but had not paid the Marconi Company patent royalties.) Com-

Statue of Tesla on Goat Island, Niagara Falls. The entrance arch of the original Niagara Falls polyphase power plant, designed by Stanford White, stands behind. (Tesla Memorial Society)

ing as it did in the middle of World War II, the decision was little
noted, but even the Supreme Court could not have unmade
Marconi's popular renown a generation after it was created.

Tesla's active wireless career foundered on the shoal of
Marconi's entrepreneurial success before the twentieth century
had fairly begun: Marconi's trans-Atlantic transmissions of
1901-02 were a public relations bonanza. Marconi undoubtedly utilized the best work of Tesla and others, but his system
was less ambitious and less expensive than Tesla's. After 1902,
Tesla was unable to raise capital to complete the giant Long
Island transmitter, modelled on his 1899 Colorado test facility,
that he had begun building in early 1901. He kept a toehold in
wireless until World War I by licensing his potentially lucrative wireless patents, but his lack of either financing or corporate ties prevented his litigating the patents effectively. Tesla
devoted most of this pre-war period to developing a simple but
powerful bladeless turbine whose success he counted on to
resurrect his wireless system; by the eve of the war, the Tesla
turbine had excited the interest of Kaiser Wilhelm, among
others. Development costs were prohibitive, however, and
post-war interest never matched pre-war expectations. The
war also aborted Tesla's last hope in the struggle with Marconi, an appeal in the French courts which some French
experts had expected to catapult the Marconi Company from
its monopoly position.[3]

My Inventions appeared during the time of the Versailles
Peace Conference — the League of Nations was obviously
much on Tesla's mind when he wrote Part VI. Tesla did not
realize how timely a moment he had chosen for a review of his
inventive career, but his period of creative glory was in fact
past, although he continued to draw on a multitude of stored
ideas. An autobiography doubtless would have been better
received two decades *before* the war, when he was at his creative peak and his wealthy publisher friend P.F. Collier was
encouraging him to make them both some money, but then he
was far too busy. Tesla was convinced of his longevity, and
often put off requests for the complete story of his life by
saying he would get to it when he was 125 and had finished his

researches. If it seems a great misfortune that his penury at half that age enforced an "early" end to his work, it is partial consolation that he used some of his free time to write about himself.

By 1919, Hugo Gernsback, publisher of the magazine *Electrical Experimenter* in which *My Inventions* appeared, had been entreating Tesla to write articles about his work for over a decade; in later years he even offered Tesla an associate editorship in hopes of getting the famous name on a magazine masthead.[4] Gernsback was enthusiastic not only because he was himself a long-time Tesla admirer, but also because he knew Tesla's name remained one to conjure with: his controversial reputation would sell magazines. Tesla's various *Electrical Experimenter* articles were very popular and created such lasting impressions on readers that even today many people think of Gernsback whenever Tesla is mentioned. Gernsback himself is best remembered as a publisher and writer of science fiction, however, and Tesla's brief but highly visible association with him may not have enhanced the inventor's reputation in the scientific community. In the two decades following the publication of *My Inventions*, Tesla came increasingly to seem a visionary 'inventor without portfolio,' given to making extravagant claims to the press. Because perceptions of him have been distorted in some unfortunate ways by this public image of his twilight years, it is useful to trace the twin roots of Tesla's reputation for controversy and his peculiar relationship with the press.

II

Tesla was always a visionary, as *My Inventions* makes clear. From the time he first captured the public's attention he rarely hesitated to make bold prophecies and ambitious claims, but because his patents quickly proved among the most valuable in history, and because he was generating new inventions at a phenomenal rate, his statements seemed amazing but entirely credible. Truth *was* more amazing than fiction in the 1890's, and Tesla was not the only man with revolutionary dreams. Perhaps not coincidentally, the decade of the 1890's was also the heyday of "yellow journalism," and the press had a field day with inventors in general and Tesla in particular. His dazzling high frequency researches and the scientific magic shows he mounted for the millionaires with whom he socialized; his many eccentricities, exotic demeanor, command of many languages and literatures, and willingness to fantasize about the shape of the future with little or no prompting, all made him a favorite with publishers like his friends Hearst and Collier.

Tesla gradually became something less of a favorite with his peers, in part because he was a loner that most of them knew only through the wild stories in the press, and in part because he was inevitably associated with the career of the "Tesla patents" long after they became sole property of the Westinghouse Corporation. Many rival inventors became bitter when they found their progress in alternating current work blocked at all turns by Westinghouse lawyers determined to prosecute — some said persecute — every conceivable patent infringer. The Westinghouse Corporation in the 1890's was weakened by the high development costs of the polyphase system as well as by the rollercoaster economics of this period of feverish American industrialization. Only by playing its trump — the Tesla patents — for maximum effect could the corporation defeat the monopolistic ambitions of General Electric. The Westinghouse strategy was successful: the apparent strength of the patents (even before they were tested in court) induced General Electric to agree to a "cross-licensing" of patents with Westinghouse. General Electric became the senior member of the partnership, but both corporations were freed to produce a complete line of equipment while smaller competitors were frozen out. (This arrangement fell afoul of the Sherman Anti-Trust Act in 1911, but by then the electrical duopoly which still dominates the United States market was well entrenched.) It is hard not to sympathize with the frustrations of gifted inventors like William Stanley, who, crushed in the middle of a corporate showdown, railed at the "patent pool trust," and reviled the name of Tesla.

The fact of the matter, of course, was that Tesla had very little to do with the Westinghouse Corporation after he sold his patents. He worked as a consultant in Pittsburgh for a year, and later gave court testimony when it was required of him, but he had no business sense nor any real interest in commercializing his work — he simply desired unlimited funds for new experiments like other inventors. For a time it appeared to the naive that Tesla's lucrative royalty agreement ($2.50 per motor horsepower) would *give* him "Rockefeller's fortune," but in 1896 Tesla became as much a pawn of the patent trust as anyone. General Electric, not in business to enrich independent inventors, made outright purchase of the Tesla patents a precondition to patent pooling, and the polyphase royalties, worth millions on paper, were signed over for $216,000. When he was questioned in court about this transaction some years later, Tesla admitted ignorance of the details of the sale — he always left such matters to his business partners![5] The powerful Tesla patents were a focus of much animosity, but Tesla himself — a perpetually abstracted man who actually seemed uncomfortable with money — was the furthest thing from a robber baron.

The public, however, rarely glimpsed the real man. In the words of Tesla's friend, science writer Kenneth Swezey, Tesla "never quite left his world, the thoughts and problems on which he was working": he often would draw sketches on tablecloths while awaiting meals, or would abruptly interrupt conversations to return to his pressing thought experiments.[6] The public knew that Tesla ate in elegant restaurants, but did not realize that his obsessions about food, and his compulsion to keep up appearances, locked him into habits he could not change no matter how destitute he became: typically, he might borrow from Peter in order to pay for Paul's dinner, and was incessantly in debt. Similarly, the public was aware of Tesla's glamorous social life — and indeed the attentions of the wealthy at first helped reassure Tesla he had "arrived" — but few people understood that Tesla was a totally driven man: he tolerated the idle pursuits of the rich primarily because he needed patrons for his ambitious projects. Finally, the public read so much hyperbolic praise of Tesla at the start of his career that their perceptions — and even *his* perceptions — of

Nikola Tesla were permanently distorted: like a gifted actor
transformed by Hollywood into a star, Tesla became a victim
of his public image. The impossible expectations of inventor
and public alike resulted in an apparent 'credibility gap' once
Tesla became unable to silence criticisms with the customary
flood of new work, and those rivals who had resented his
earlier success were quick to emphasize how the mighty had
fallen.

Reginald Kapp, whose father Gisbert was Tesla's friend
and peer, once observed that "Tesla presents an interesting
study of the way in which a man's personality may both
generate his intellectual achievements and set a limit to
them,"[7] an ironic situation common among inventors. The
same passionate conviction that mesmerized millionaires, the
same stubbornness that shed conventional wisdom and made
Tesla a great, not just a good inventor, and the same relentless
optimism that kept him bouncing back from the edge of despair
also prevented him from recognizing his own errors, and
ultimately drove him to invest himself most heavily exactly
where he was most doomed to fail. Tesla always projected
supreme self-confidence, aggravating less sanguine inventors
who little suspected how this role trapped him into making
ever-greater demands on himself as his fortunes faltered. Tesla
had a need for recognition that *My Inventions* shows to be
deeply rooted in childhood, and he was paradoxically capable
of deploring his sensationalized press coverage one moment,
and fostering it with startling predictions and promises the
next. The technical press, although loath to dismiss Tesla's
claims outright because of his formidable reputation, began to
insist that he more concretely support them. The popular
press was more forgiving, however: Tesla the controversial
visionary could sell newspapers and magazines just as fast as
Tesla the scientific superman ever had.

III

The turning point in Tesla's relations with the press
came in June, 1900, with his publication of "The Problem of

Increasing Human Energy."[8] Tesla returned to New York in 1900 having exhausted all of his funds on his Colorado wireless researches. Hoping to attract new money for a projected "World System" of wireless power and message transmission, he arranged with his friend Robert Johnson, editor of the *Century* magazine, to print a lengthy article on his recent work. Johnson had been instrumental during the 1890's in introducing Tesla to millionaire investors, most of whom were predisposed to admire the inventor because of the stranglehold the "Tesla patents" had on alternating current technology. The *Century* article represented Tesla's first completely intentional effort to use the power of the press to raise money; to that end he studded the article with photographs of spectacular electrical discharges that still evoke wonder today, even when it is realized that the photographs are time exposures showing many different discharges. The article was as successful as Tesla could have hoped: J.P. Morgan was sufficiently impressed to invest $150,000 in Tesla's wireless system.

"The Problem of Increasing Human Energy" also aroused considerable controversy, however. Despite Robert Johnson's plea to "give us an informing article and not a metaphysical one,"[9] Tesla devoted little space to concrete descriptions of his wireless work, and entire sections to expansive plans for remaking the world along scientific, energy-efficient lines. Tesla delighted in pushing his mechanistic theories of life to their logical extremes — not only was each man an automaton, but mankind as a whole obeyed the laws of physics just as surely as gas molecules obey the 'gas laws.' (At the beginning of World War I Tesla calculated with startling accuracy the duration of the war by extrapolating from previous wars according to his theories.[10]) Tesla's efforts to divine the future through a bold, poetic synthesis of history, philosophy, and science met the same fate as similar efforts by his near-contemporary, the free-thinking historian Henry Adams (grandson of John Quincy Adams).[11] Both men were labelled by a literal-minded world as, at best, eccentric, or at worst, as unfaithful to the rules of their professions. Yet today, the world actually pulses with electrical intelligence and power

'like a living organism,' much as Tesla predicted it would
with his "World System." Opinion is still divided whether
Adams' vision of destruction or Tesla's of salvation by technology is more plausible, but ambitious, cross-disciplinary
attempts to read the future are no longer dismissed as unpro-
fessional: the pace of technological and societal change has
become so rapid that futuristic thinking may hold our only
hope of keeping pace.

Tesla did not wade into the "Human Energy" controversy unaware; his letters indicate that he expected criticism of
both his futuristic ideas and his "World System" claims. He
was playing for high stakes — as Marconi biographer Orrin
Dunlap observed, Tesla might well have become the "father of
radio" in the eyes of the public instead of Marconi.[12] Tesla was
gambling his reputation, much as Edison had once gambled
his by proclaiming in the most spectacular terms the success of
his lighting system before it had even operated in the lab.
Extravagant claims are often a necessary part of entrepreneur-
ship — they attract criticism but also investors. Like Edison
and Marconi, Tesla had total confidence in his untested new
system, but unlike them he was not a natural entrepreneur.
Marconi knew himself to be in a race to perfect radio, and
predicated his every action on its advertising value. By con-
trast, Tesla wanted to unveil his completed "World System"
one morning and have all competitors retire defeated from the
field. His polyphase success had been quick and sweeping, he
had easily attracted venture capital from his millionaire
acquaintances, and he could invent rings around Marconi.
Marconi, of course, was smart enough to surround himself
with talented people, but what ultimately doomed Tesla was
his own limitless ambition. Marconi wanted only to send
messages, but Tesla's real purpose (disguised from J.P. Morgan, who must have looked at the *Century* article's pictures
without reading the text) was to wirelessly electrify the entire
earth, instantaneously making available to the world's remot-
est hamlet all the benefits of the electrical age, free for the
taking! Tesla was so intent on this utopian goal that he hardly
bothered to publicize his wirelessly-controlled boat, which in

1898 was years ahead of the devices of his radio and robotics competitors.

Whatever one thinks of the practicality of Tesla's plans to rhythmically 'disturb the electrical condition' of the earth, making power available everywhere, it is a pity that he was never able to fully test it, after having come tantalizingly close to completing his huge Long Island transmitter. Tesla never completely recovered from watching his favorite "child" suffer slow financial starvation. After an initial period of severe depression, he recovered the semblance of his former positivism, and recommenced inventing, but he never gave up hoping to revive his greatest project. Considering Tesla's roots in the mid-nineteenth century, this fixation on the lost opportunities of the past, which so impeded his acceptance of and by twentieth-century science, hardly seems surprising —few men can be avant-garde in successive centuries. *My Inventions* shows Tesla still remarkably ready, at age 63, to laugh at his own grandiose ambitions, but by the end of his long life his visionary predilections, weakness for the press, and longing to recreate past triumphs had eroded this perspective. Tesla's final years were marked by startling announcements of perpetual energy machines and ultimate weapons that apparently never existed outside of his mind, and whose workability it is therefore impossible to judge. Perhaps he thought he could use the newspapers to galvanize public attention as he once had used the *Century* magazine, but — never having learned the perils to amateur publicists of trying to play the press — he succeeded mainly in making himself a newspaper oddity, a colorful relic from the already distant nineteenth century. Ultimately, Tesla and the press settled into a familiar yearly ritual, wherein the inventor invited reporters to a lavish birthday dinner he could ill afford, and regaled them with schemes more visionary than those of the year before. Tesla outlived most of his contemporaries, and followed the pattern of other great inventors: old age only reinforced the stubbornness that had, in youth, enabled him to withstand the world's unanimous doubts and overturn its conventional wisdom.

IV

It is to Tesla's youth that one must look to find the seeds of his creativity, although Tesla's most ardent admirers and detractors alike tend to focus on the imaginative flights of his old age. (Detractors cite these as the fantasies of a hopeless dreamer, while admirers regard them as the inspirations of an infallible prophet.) Fortunately, Tesla in *My Inventions* places particular emphasis on his youthful experiences as determinants of all that followed, and his irreplaceable and fascinating testimony has been a primary source for all Tesla biographers. However, Tesla's focus in *My Inventions* is primarily an interior one, and readers need some sense of the historical and geographical context of his childhood. He was born of Serbian parents in Croatia, was educated in Croatian, Austrian and Czech schools, and found his first engineering job in Hungary — many different groups have proudly claimed him for their own. His native Lika (pronounced 'Leeka'), in the Croatian republic of what is today Yugoslavia (land of the south or 'yugo' Slavs), was long part of the Austrian Empire's Military Frontier, a militarized zone that stretched a thousand miles along the empire's border with the Turkish (Ottoman) empire to the south and east. A majority of the Frontier's residents were southern Slavs — Serbs, Croats (Croh-ahts), Slovenes — and almost all of its men were life-long soldiers who might at any time be sent off to fight distant wars. The Frontier was expected to be self-supporting, but because the men had numerous army duties even in peacetime, farming often became the province of women and children. Lika, a mountainous and infertile karst region perpetually at the edge of famine (it remains today one of the poorest parts of Yugoslavia) produced some of the Frontier's toughest and most resourceful men and women.

The Frontier was hundreds of years old at Tesla's birth, and changes in warfare, as well as the wane of Turkish power, had finally made it obsolete. It was returning to civilian administration when Tesla reached draft age, and as a result Tesla saw his military obligation (never mentioned in *My*

A modern map of the regions of Tesla's childhood and school years. In Tesla's youth, Austria-Hungary controlled Croatia and the lands north of the Sava river, while Turkey ruled Bosnia and the lands to the south. Austria's Military Frontier incorporated a wide belt of Croatia, beginning on the mountainous Adriatic coast south of Gospić, and running north and then east along the boundary between Croatia and Bosnia.

Inventions) reduced from sixty-four to a mere three years; Tesla in fact avoided the army altogether by enrolling in technical school. Tesla was fortunate in other ways: his father was a Serbian Orthodox priest and an educated man (the two were not necessarily synonymous at that time); his mother came from a distinguished clerical (Serbian Orthodox) family; and many maternal and paternal relatives were influential priests or military officers. Moreover, the Frontier, which had so long stagnated as an Austrian military zone, had had its horizons immensely broadened by the brief Napoleonic occupation during Tesla's grandfather's time. Europe had flowered in the centuries since the Turkish invasions had been checked, but the Frontier, trapped between East and West, had remained a complete hostage of the past until the modern army and modern ideas of Napoleonic France swept through. Although Tesla was himself born into a repressive period which immediately followed the great European revolutions of mid-century, the winds of change were not easily smothered, and the young and ambitious Tesla took advantage of them to sail away to a newer world.

In *My Inventions,* Tesla only alludes to most of the ancient traditions that he left so far behind. He was steeped in the heroic oral literature with which the South Slavs commemorated their almost timeless battles against Islamic invaders, and he grew up amidst one of the world's most complex geo-political situations — one such as only millennia of wars, migrations, and imperial edicts, acting on a tapestry of different cultures, races and religions, can produce. Many ancient tensions remain today — Catholic, Orthodox, or Moslem; German, Hungarian or Slav; Serb, Croat, or Albanian: each group must co-exist with the others but is hindered by memories of old conflicts and the need to retain a cultural identity. The Balkans are perched, as ever, between competing empires (although the names have changed) and Islam is once again casting a long shadow into Europe. These influences on Tesla, ignored in *My Inventions,* are unfortunately far too complex to be developed here, but they certainly deserve study by anyone desiring to understand Tesla's world better.

Finally, it must be observed that Tesla's interior focus in *My Inventions* gives the reader an incomplete picture not only of Tesla's surroundings, but also of the childhood experiences which he recognizes as being so important. Autobiographies almost by definition leave out many of the most critical parts of a person's life, parts he or she cannot see clearly or perhaps would rather forget. It is imperative for serious students of Tesla's life to give *My Inventions* a very close reading, and where there seem to be omissions or discrepancies, to seek out secondary sources. European writers have done some insightful detective work concerning Tesla's early life, but American biographers, more fascinated by Tesla's glamorous American period than his difficult formative years, have uniformly contented themselves with unimaginative digests of *My Inventions.* This writer's own views on the subject of Tesla's early life, developed in the biography, *And In Creating, Live*, will not be detailed here; Tesla should be afforded the right to tell his own story, and readers the right to form their own opinions, before extensive interpretation is entered into.

V

Unfortunately for the many readers already familiar with either John O'Neill's 1944 biography of Tesla, *Prodigal Genius*, or later biographical accounts derived from it, approaching Tesla's autobiography without preconceptions is difficult, if not impossible. O'Neill admired Tesla and had the benefit of several good sources (including Tesla's nephew Sava Kosanovich), but his book has been primarily responsible for much of the mythology that today surrounds Tesla's name. *Prodigal Genius* is a mixture of fact and fiction, with few footnotes and no bibliography to help the reader differentiate between the two.* Any books or articles which cite O'Neill as a source must be approached very cautiously; furthermore, the reader of *My Inventions* must pay particular attention to passages that seem confusing or surprising in light of what he or she may already know — O'Neill's version of events, which permeates so much of what people *think* they know about Tesla, could be intruding unbidden.

*O'Neill prepared a partial bibliography which was never published. A copy exists in the Smithsonian's Swezey file. (See footnote 4)

An excellent example of how a myth, once given birth, can perpetuate itself indefinitely, is the story of Tesla's "prevision" of his mother's death, told in *Prodigal Genius* and repeated in every American biography since.[13] O'Neill was a fervent spiritualist who was convinced that Tesla had psychic powers, although Tesla himself wrote in *My Inventions* that he only *once* had an experience that he for a time thought might be "supernatural." This was a vision of his mother on a cloud full of angelic figures which came to him (p. 104) at about the time of her death. Tesla was then bedridden (not far from his mother) *himself,* having been overcome by the strain of lecturing in Europe, next rushing home "without an hour's rest," and finally, attending his mother's bedside during her last weeks of life. Some time after her death, when he had recovered his equilibrium, Tesla rationally explained the vision to himself (p. 105), but O'Neill apparently never accepted this explanation. When Tesla had died and could not protest, O'Neill invented *another* supernatural episode — the "prevision" story — and made it the centerpiece of his case for Tesla's psychic abilities.

Many of the errors in *Prodigal Genius* can be attributed to O'Neill's rush to get into print — he was in failing health yet was determined to publish America's first Tesla biography. In the case of the "prevision" story, however, he deliberately *edited* a passage of *My Inventions* (pp. 94-95) to make it seem that Tesla saw in advance his mother's death and the events surrounding it. Tesla actually described a "post-vision," which took place at the climax of an amnesiac episode sometime after his mother's death in 1892. (On page 94 he says the episode grew out of his exhaustion from struggling with his grounded transmitter, while on page 106 he says he only began his wireless investigations in 1893.*) Tesla's account is very clear to

---

*Tesla's lectures and correspondence indicate that wireless was in the back of his mind in 1892, and moved to the forefront only after his mother's death. A December 17, 1934 letter to George Viereck, abstracted (with selected quotations) in the New York Public Library's Tesla collection, clearly states that Tesla's breakdown came "after evolving my system of wireless transmission of energy."

anyone who has not read O'Neill's version first: Tesla describes how he forgot all of his previous existence except earliest infancy, and how his memory returned only gradually, working its way forward in time. Ultimately, the peculiar nervous breakdown he was experiencing climaxed as had the previous one: Tesla underwent the tremendous "pain and distress" of witnessing his mother's death for a second time! O'Neill quotes Tesla's description of this trauma verbatim from *My Inventions*, but disguises his source* and deletes the one sentence that clearly placed Tesla's mother's death in the past and not the future: "I remembered how I made the long journey home without an hour of rest and how she passed away after weeks of agony!" (O'Neill poetically compressed to a single evening the six weeks separating Tesla's return home in February and his mother's death in April![14]) So many writers have now repeated O'Neill's and each other's versions of this "prevision" story that Tesla's fascinating and revealing account of amnesia has been totally submerged in a sea of mystical speculation.

In *My Inventions*, Tesla mentions his exasperation at being adopted by devotees of the supernatural. He was generally very skeptical about psychic phenomena, despite his childhood exposure to the endemic superstition of Lika and his adult admiration for the British scientist and psychic researcher William Crookes. In combination with all of Tesla's misadventures with journalists (and in death, biographers) the unsought association with the supernatural had by mid-twentieth century clouded Tesla's reputation. Fortunately, however, the indefatigable educational efforts of the late Kenneth Swezey and other Tesla admirers have regained for Tesla's name the respect it once commanded.[15] In 1956, the cente-

---

*O'Neill called his source an "unpublished manuscript," probably to evade the copyright. He could get away with this deception, repeated several times in *Prodigal Genius*, because Hugo Gernsback's Experimenter Publishing Company, holder of the copyright, had passed into new ownership in 1929. Gernsback, a great Tesla admirer who would undoubtedly have read *Prodigal Genius*, must have been aware of the copyright infringement, but no longer had any financial interest in the matter.

nary of Tesla's birth, the unit of magnetic flux density in the worldwide Système International (meter-kilogram-second) of measurements was named in his honor. The American engineering establishment now numbers him among its greatest alumni, no small honor for a man of foreign birth. It is to be hoped that reissuing Tesla's autobiography may, in this time of renewed interest in his career, help dispel some of the lingering misconceptions that even today make Tesla the subject of sensationalist journalism and the object of cult worship. Tesla and his public both deserve much better.

Ben Johnston

FOOTNOTES

1. Nikola Tesla, "A New System of Alternate Current Motors and Transformers," *Transactions of the American Institute of Electrical Engineers,* Vol. 5, pp. 308-324, July, 1888.

2. *United States Reports,* Cases Adjudged in the Supreme Court, Vol. 320 (October Term, 1942); Marconi Wireless Telegraph Company of America v. United States, pp. 1-80.

3. Emile Girardeau, "Pourquoi Nikola Tesla, Créateur de la Radio-Electricité, A-t-il Eté Longtemps Méconnu?", address originally delivered in Belgrade, 1938. Reprinted in *Tribute to Nikola Tesla,* Belgrade, 1961.

4. Letter, Hugo Gernsback to Tesla, May 25, 1929, Tesla Museum, Belgrade. Excerpted in Kenneth Swezey collection, Smithsonian Institution.

5. Letter, Kenneth Swezey to Royal Lee, April 15, 1956, Smithsonian Institution.

6. Alexander Nenadović, "The Centenary of Tesla's Birth," *Politika,* Belgrade, July 8, 1956, p. 680. (Translation from Serbo-Croatian.)

7. Letter, Reginald Kapp to Kenneth Swezey, Sept. 2, 1958, Smithsonian Institution.

8. Nikola Tesla, "The Problem of Increasing Human Energy," *Century* magazine, June, 1900, pp. 175-211.

9. Microfilm letter, Robert Johnson to Tesla, March 6, 1900, Library of Congress. (Original in Tesla Museum.)

10. Nikola Tesla, "Science and Discovery are the Great Forces Which Will Lead to the Consummation of the War," *New York Sun,* Dec. 20, 1914.

11. Henry Adams, "A Dynamic Theory of History" in *The Education of Henry Adams,* New York, 1918, and "The Rule of Phase Applied to History" in *The Degradation of the Democratic Dogma,* New York, 1919, among other essays.

12. Orrin E. Dunlap, Jr., *Marconi, The Man and His Wireless,* New York, 1937, p. 33.

13. John J. O'Neill, *Prodigal Genius,* New York, 1944, pp. 264-265.

14. Ibid., p. 101.

15. Kenneth Swezey, "Nikola Tesla," *Science,* May 16, 1958, pp. 1147-1158.

MY INVENTIONS

Dr. Tesla, still youthful at 63.

I. MY EARLY LIFE

THE progressive development of man is vitally dependent on invention. It is the most important product of his creative brain. Its ultimate purpose is the complete mastery of mind over the material world, the harnessing of the forces of nature to human needs. This is the difficult task of the inventor who is often misunderstood and unrewarded. But he finds ample compensation in the pleasing exercises of his powers and in the knowledge of being one of that exceptionally privileged class without whom the race would have long ago perished in the bitter struggle against pitiless elements.

Speaking for myself, I have already had more than my full measure of this exquisite enjoyment, so much that for many years my life was little short of continuous rapture. I am credited with being one of the hardest workers and perhaps I am, if thought is the equivalent of labor, for I have devoted to it almost all of my waking hours. But if work is interpreted to be a definite performance in a specified time according to a rigid rule, then I may be the worst of idlers. Every effort under compulsion demands a sacrifice of life-energy. I never paid such a price. On the contrary, I have thrived on my thoughts.

In attempting to give a connected and faithful account of my activities in this series of articles which will be presented with the assistance of the Editors of the ELECTRICAL EXPERIMENTER and are chiefly addrest to our young men readers, I must dwell, however reluctantly, on the impressions of my youth and the circumstances and events which have been instrumental in determining my career.

Our first endeavors are purely instinctive, promptings of an imagination vivid and undisciplined. As we grow older reason asserts itself and we become more and more systematic and designing. But those early impulses, tho not immediately productive, are of the greatest moment and may shape our very destinies. Indeed, I feel now that had I understood and cultivated instead of suppressing them, I would have added substantial value to my bequest to the world. But not until I had attained manhood did I realize that I was an inventor.

This was due to a number of causes. In the first place I had a brother who was gifted to an extraordinary degree — one of those rare phenomena of mentality which biological investigation has failed to explain. His premature death left my parents disconsolate. We owned a horse which had been presented to us by a dear friend. It was a magnificent animal of Arabian breed, possest of almost human intelligence, and was cared for and petted by the whole family, having on one occasion saved my father's life under remarkable circumstances. My father had been called one winter night to perform an urgent duty and while crossing the mountains, infested by wolves, the horse became frightened and ran away, throwing him violently to the ground. It arrived home bleeding and exhausted, but after the alarm was sounded immediately dashed off again, returning to the spot, and before the searching party were far on the way they were met by my father, who had recovered consciousness and remounted, not realizing that he had been lying in the snow for several hours. This horse was responsible for my brother's injuries from which he died. I witnest the tragic scene and altho fifty-six years have elapsed since, my visual impression of it has lost none of its force. The recollection of his attainments made every effort of mine seem dull in comparison.

Anything I did that was creditable merely caused my parents to feel their loss more keenly. So I grew up with little confidence in myself. But I was far from being considered a stupid boy, if I am to judge from an incident of which I have still a strong remembrance. One day the Aldermen were passing thru a street where I was at play with other boys. The oldest of these venerable gentlemen — a wealthy citizen — paused to give a silver piece to each of us. Coming to me he suddenly stopt and commanded, "Look in my eyes." I met his gaze, my hand outstretched to receive the much valued coin, when, to my dismay, he said, "No, not much, you can get nothing from me, you are too smart." They used to tell a funny story about me. I had two old aunts with wrinkled faces, one of them having two teeth protruding like the tusks of an elephant which she buried in my cheek every time she kist me. Nothing would scare me more than the prospect of being hugged by these as affectionate as unattractive relatives. It happened that while being carried in my mother's arms they asked me who was the prettier of the two. After examining their faces intently, I answered thoughtfully, pointing to one of them, "This here is not as ugly as the other."

Then again, I was intended from my very birth for the clerical profession and this thought constantly opprest me. I longed to be an engineer but my father was inflexible. He was the son of an officer who served in the army of the Great Napoleon and, in common with his brother, professor of mathematics in a prominent institution, had received a military education but, singularly enough, later embraced the clergy in which vocation he achieved eminence. He was a very erudite man, a veritable natural philosopher, poet and writer and his sermons were said to be as eloquent as those of Abraham a Sancta-Clara. He had a prodigious memory and frequently recited at length from works in several languages. He often remarked playfully that if some of the classics were lost he could restore them. His style of writing was much admired. He penned sentences short and terse and was full of wit and satire. The humorous remarks he made were always peculiar and characteristic. Just to illustrate, I may mention one or two instances. Among the help there was a cross-eyed man called Mane, employed to do work around the farm. He was chopping wood one day. As he swung the axe my father, who stood nearby and felt very uncomfortable, cautioned him, "For

God's sake, Mane, do not strike at what you are looking but at what you intend to hit." On another occasion he was taking out for a drive a friend who carelessly permitted his costly fur coat to rub on the carriage wheel. My father reminded him of it saying, "Pull in your coat, you are ruining my tire." He had the odd habit of talking to himself and would often carry on an animated conversation and indulge in heated argument, changing the tone of his voice. A casual listener might have sworn that several people were in the room.

Altho I must trace to my mother's influence whatever inventiveness I possess, the training he gave me must have been helpful. It comprised all sorts of exercises — as, guessing one another's thoughts, discovering the defects of some form or expression, repeating long sentences or performing mental calculations. These daily lessons were intended to strengthen memory and reason and especially to develop the critical sense, and were undoubtedly very beneficial.

My mother descended from one of the oldest families in the country and a line of inventors. Both her father and grand-father originated numerous implements for household, agricultural and other uses. She was a truly great woman, of rare skill, courage and fortitude, who had braved the storms of life and past thru many a trying experience. When she was sixteen a virulent pestilence swept the country. Her father was called away to administer the last sacraments to the dying and during his absence she went alone to the assistance of a neighboring family who were stricken by the dread disease. All of the members, five in number, succumbed in rapid succession. She bathed, clothed and laid out the bodies, decorating them with flowers according to the custom of the country and when her father returned he found everything ready for a Christian burial. My mother was an inventor of the first order and would, I believe, have achieved great things had she not been so remote from modern life and its multifold opportunities. She invented and constructed all kinds of tools and devices and wove the finest designs from thread which was spun by her. She even planted the seeds, raised the plants and separated the fibers herself. She worked indefatigably, from break of day till late at night, and most of the wearing apparel and furnishings of the home was the product of her hands. When she was past sixty, her fingers were still nimble enough *to tie three knots in an eyelash.*

There was another and still more important reason for my late awakening. In my boyhood I suffered from a peculiar affliction due to the appearance of images, often accompanied by strong flashes of light, which marred the sight of real objects and interfered with my thought and action. They were pictures of things and scenes which I had really seen, never of those I imagined. When a word was spoken to me the image of the object it designated would present itself vividly to my vision and sometimes I was quite unable to distinguish whether what I saw was tangible or not. This caused me great discomfort and anxiety. None of the students of psychology or physiology whom I have consulted could ever explain satisfactorily these phenomena. They seem to have been unique altho I was probably predisposed as I know that my brother experienced a similar trouble. The theory I have formulated is that the images were the result of a reflex action from the brain

Nikola Tesla's birthplace at Smiljan in Lika, a province of Croatia. (The ruins of his father's church are on the right.) Tesla's native region is today part of Yugoslavia, but at his birth it was still governed as a military district by Austria-Hungary. (Smithsonian Institution)

on the retina under great excitation. They certainly were not hallucinations such as are produced in diseased and anguished minds, for in other respects I was normal and composed. To give an idea of my distress, suppose that I had witnest a funeral or some such nerve-racking spectacle. Then, inevitably, in the stillness of night, a vivid picture of the scene would thrust itself *before* my eyes and persist despite all my efforts to banish it. Sometimes it would even remain fixt in space tho I pushed my hand thru it. If my explanation is correct, it should be possible to project on a screen the image of any object one conceives and make it visible. Such an advance would revolutionize all human relations. I am convinced that this wonder can and will be accomplished in time to come; I may add that I have devoted much thought to the solution of the problem.

To free myself of these tormenting appearances, I tried to concentrate my mind on something else I had seen, and in this way I would often obtain temporary relief; but in order to get it I had to conjure continuously new images. It was not long before I found that I had exhausted all of those at my command; my "reel" had run out, as it were, because I had seen little of the world — only objects in my home and the immediate surroundings. As I performed these mental operations for the second or third time, in order to chase the appearances from my vision, the remedy gradually lost all its force. Then I instinctively commenced to make excursions beyond the limits of the small world of which I had knowledge, and I saw new scenes. These were at first very blurred and indistinct, and would flit away when I tried to concentrate my attention upon them, but by and by I succeeded in fixing them; they gained in strength and distinctness and finally assumed the concreteness of real things. I soon discovered that my best comfort was attained if I simply went on in my vision farther and farther, getting new impressions all the time, and so I began to travel — of course, in my mind. Every night (and sometimes during the day), when alone, I would start on my journeys — see new places, cities and countries — live there, meet people and make friendships and acquaintances and, however unbelievable, it is a fact that they were just as dear to me as those in actual life and not a bit less intense in their manifestations.

This I did constantly until I was about seventeen when my thoughts turned seriously to invention. Then I observed to my delight that I could visualize with the greatest facility. I needed no models, drawings or experiments. I could picture them all as real in my mind. Thus I have been led unconsciously to evolve what I consider a new method of materializing inventive concepts and ideas, which is radically opposite to the purely experimental and is in my opinion ever so much more expeditious and efficient. The moment one constructs a device to carry into practise a crude idea he finds himself unavoidably engrost with the details and defects of the apparatus. As he goes on improving and reconstructing, his force of concentration diminishes and he loses sight of the great underlying principle. Results may be obtained but always at the sacrifice of quality.

My method is different. I do not rush into actual work. When I get an idea I start at once building it up in my imagination. I change the construction, make improvements and operate the device in my mind. It is absolutely immaterial to me whether I run my turbine in thought or test it in my shop. *I even note if it is out of balance.* There is no difference whatever, the results are the same. In this way I am able to rapidly develop and perfect a conception without touching anything. When I have gone so far as to embody in the invention every possible improvement I can think of and see no fault anywhere, I put into concrete form this final product of my brain. Invariably my device works as I conceived that it should, and the experiment comes out exactly as I planned it. In twenty years there has not been a single exception. Why should it be otherwise? Engineering, electrical and mechanical, is positive in results. There is scarcely a subject that cannot be mathematically treated and the effects calculated or the results determined beforehand from the available theoretical and practical data. The carrying out into practise of a crude idea as is being generally done is, I hold, nothing but a waste of energy, money and time.

My early affliction had, however, another compensation.

The incessant mental exertion developed my powers of observation and enabled me to discover a truth of great importance.
I had noted that the appearance of images was always preceded
by actual vision of scenes under peculiar and generally very
exceptional conditions and I was impelled on each occasion to
locate the original impulse. After a while this effort grew to be
almost automatic and I gained great facility in connecting
cause and effect. Soon I became aware, to my surprise, that
every thought I conceived was suggested by an external
impression. Not only this but all my actions were prompted in
a similar way. In the course of time it became perfectly evident
to me that I was merely an *automaton* endowed with power of
movement, responding to the stimuli of the sense organs and
thinking and acting accordingly. The practical result of this
was the art of *telautomatics* which has been so far carried out
only in an imperfect manner. Its latent possibilities will, however, be eventually shown. I have been since years planning
self-controlled automata and believe that mechanisms can be
produced which will act as if possest of reason, to a limited
degree, and will create a revolution in many commercial and
industrial departments.

    I was about twelve years old when I first succeeded in
banishing an image from my vision by wilful effort, but I
never had any control over the flashes of light to which I have
referred. They were, perhaps, my strangest experience and
inexplicable. They usually occurred when I found myself in a
dangerous or distressing situation or when I was greatly exhil-
arated. In some instances I have seen all the air around me
filled with tongues of living flame. Their intensity, instead of
diminishing, increased with time and seemingly attained a
maximum when I was about twenty-five years old. While in
Paris, in 1883, a prominent French manufacturer sent me an
invitation to a shooting expedition which I accepted. I had
been long confined to the factory and the fresh air had a
wonderfully invigorating effect on me. On my return to the
city that night I felt a positive sensation that my brain had
caught fire. I saw a light as tho a small sun was located in it
and I past the whole night applying cold compressions to my
tortured head. Finally the flashes diminished in frequency and

force but it took more than three weeks before they wholly subsided. When a second invitation was extended to me my answer was an emphatic NO!

These luminous phenomena still manifest themselves from time to time, as when a new idea opening up possibilities strikes me, but they are no longer exciting, being of relatively small intensity. When I close my eyes I invariably observe first, a background of very dark and uniform blue, not unlike the sky on a clear but starless night. In a few seconds this field becomes animated with innumerable scintillating flakes of green, arranged in several layers and advancing towards me. Then there appears, to the right, a beautiful pattern of two systems of parallel and closely spaced lines, at right angles to one another, in all sorts of colors with yellow-green and gold predominating. Immediately thereafter the lines grow brighter and the whole is thickly sprinkled with dots of twinkling light. This picture moves slowly across the field of vision and in about ten seconds vanishes to the left, leaving behind a ground of rather unpleasant and inert grey which quickly gives way to a billowy sea of clouds, seemingly trying to mould themselves in living shapes. It is curious that I cannot project a form into this grey until the second phase is reached. Every time, before falling asleep, images of persons or objects flit before my view. When I see them I know that I am about to lose consciousness. If they are absent and refuse to come it means a sleepless night.

To what an extent imagination played a part in my early life I may illustrate by another odd experience. Like most children I was fond of jumping and developed an intense desire to support myself in the air. Occasionally a strong wind richly charged with oxygen blew from the mountains rendering my body as light as cork and then I would leap and float in space for a long time. It was a delightful sensation and my disappointment was keen when later I undeceived myself.

During that period I contracted many strange likes, dislikes and habits, some of which I can trace to external impressions while others are unaccountable. I had a violent aversion against the earrings of women but other ornaments, as bracelets, pleased me more or less according to design. The sight of

a pearl would almost give me a fit but I was fascinated with
the glitter of crystals or objects with sharp edges and plane
surfaces. I would not touch the hair of other people except,
perhaps, at the point of a revolver. I would get a fever by
looking at a peach and if a piece of camphor was anywhere in
the house it caused me the keenest discomfort. Even now I am
not insensible to some of these upsetting impulses. When I
drop little squares of paper in a dish filled with liquid, I
always sense a peculiar and awful taste in my mouth. I counted
the steps in my walks and calculated the cubical contents of
soup plates, coffee cups and pieces of food — otherwise my
meal was unenjoyable. All repeated acts or operations I performed had to be divisible by three and if I mist I felt impelled
to do it all over again, even if it took hours.

Up to the age of eight years, my character was weak and
vacillating. I had neither courage or strength to form a firm
resolve. My feelings came in waves and surges and vibrated
unceasingly between extremes. My wishes were of consuming
force and like the heads of the hydra, they multiplied. I was
opprest by thoughts of pain in life and death and religious
fear. I was swayed by superstitious belief and lived in constant
dread of the spirit of evil, of ghosts and ogres and other unholy
monsters of the dark. Then, all at once, there came a tremendous change which altered the course of my whole existence.

Of all things I liked books the best. My father had a large
library and whenever I could manage I tried to satisfy my
passion for reading. He did not permit it and would fly into a
rage when he caught me in the act. He hid the candles when he
found that I was reading in secret. He did not want me to spoil
my eyes. But I obtained tallow, made the wicking and cast the
sticks into tin forms, and every night I would bush the keyhole
and the cracks and read, often till dawn, when all others slept
and my mother started on her arduous daily task. On one
occasion I came across a novel entitled "Abafi" (the Son of
Aba), a Serbian translation of a well known Hungarian writer,
Josika. This work somehow awakened my dormant powers of
will and I began to practise self-control. At first my resolutions
faded like snow in April, but in a little while I conquered my
weakness and felt a pleasure I never knew before — that of

doing as I willed. In the course of time this vigorous mental exercise became second nature. At the outset my wishes had to be subdued but gradually desire and will grew to be identical. After years of such discipline I gained so complete a mastery over myself that I toyed with passions which have meant destruction to some of the strongest men. At a certain age I contracted a mania for gambling which greatly worried my parents. To sit down to a game of cards was for me the quintessence of pleasure. My father led an exemplary life and could not excuse the senseless waste of time and money in which I indulged. I had a strong resolve but my philosophy was bad. I would say to him, "I can stop whenever I please but is it worth while to give up that which I would purchase with the joys of Paradise?" On frequent occasions he gave vent to his anger and contempt but my mother was different. She understood the character of men and knew that one's salvation could only be brought about thru his own efforts. One afternoon, I remember, when I had lost all my money and was craving for a game, she came to me with a roll of bills and said, "Go and enjoy yourself. The sooner you lose all we possess the better it will be. I know that you will get over it." She was right. I conquered my passion then and there and only regretted that it had not been a hundred times as strong. I not only vanquished but tore it from my heart so as not to leave even a trace of desire. Ever since that time I have been as indifferent to any form of gambling as to picking teeth.

During another period I smoked excessively, threatening to ruin my health. Then my will asserted itself and I not only stopt but destroyed all inclination. Long ago I suffered from heart trouble until I discovered that it was due to the innocent cup of coffee I consumed every morning. I discontinued at once, tho I confess it was not an easy task. In this way I checked and bridled other habits and passions and have not only preserved my life but derived an immense amount of satisfaction from what most men would consider privation and sacrifice.

After finishing the studies at the Polytechnic Institute and University I had a complete nervous breakdown and while the malady lasted I observed many phenomena strange and unbelievable.

Nikola Tesla at the age of 23.

II. MY FIRST EFFORTS
IN INVENTION

I SHALL dwell briefly on these extraordinary experiences, on account of their possible interest to students of psychology and physiology and also because this period of agony was of the greatest consequence on my mental development and subsequent labors. But it is indispensable to first relate the circumstances and conditions which preceded them and in which might be found their partial explanation.

From childhood I was compelled to concentrate attention upon myself. This caused me much suffering but, to my present view, it was a blessing in disguise for it has taught me to appreciate the inestimable value of introspection in the preservation of life, as well as a means of achievement. The pressure of occupation and the incessant stream of impressions pouring into our consciousness thru all the gateways of knowledge make modern existence hazardous in many ways. Most persons are so absorbed in the contemplation of the outside world that they are wholly oblivious to what is passing on within themselves. The premature death of millions is primarily traceable to this cause. Even among those who exercise care it is a common mistake to avoid imaginary, and ignore the real dangers. And what is true of an individual also applies, more or less, to a people as a whole. Witness, in illustration, the prohibition movement. A drastic, if not unconstitutional, measure is now being put thru in this country to prevent the consumption of alcohol and yet it is a positive fact that coffee, tea, tobacco, chewing gum and other stimulants, which are freely indulged in even at the tender age, are vastly more injurious to the national body, judging from the number of those who succumb. So, for instance, during my student years I gathered from the published necrologues in Vienna, the home of coffee drinkers, that deaths from heart trouble sometimes reached *sixty-seven per cent* of the total. Similar observations might probably be made in cities where the consumption of tea is excessive. These delicious beverages superexcite and gradually exhaust the fine fibers of the brain. They also interfere seriously with arterial circulation and should be enjoyed all the more sparingly as their deleterious effects are slow and imperceptible. Tobacco, on the other hand, is conducive to easy and pleasant thinking and detracts from the intensity and concentration necessary to all original and vigorous effort of the intellect. Chewing gum is helpful for a short while but soon drains the glandular system and inflicts irreparable damage, not to speak of the revulsion it creates. Alcohol in small quantities is an excellent tonic, but is toxic in its action when absorbed in larger amounts, quite immaterial as to whether it is taken in as whiskey or produced in the stomach from sugar. But it should not be overlooked that all these are great eliminators assisting Nature, as they do, in upholding her stern but just law of the survival of the fittest. Eager reformers should also be mindful of the eternal perversity of mankind which makes the indifferent *"laissez-faire"* by far preferable to enforced restraint. The truth about this is that we need stimulants to do our best work under present living conditions, and that we must exercise moderation and control our appetites and inclinations in every direction. That is what I have been doing for many years, in this way maintaining myself young in body and mind. Abstinence was not always to my liking but I find ample reward in the agreeable experiences I am now making. Just in the hope of converting some to my precepts and convictions I will recall one or two.

A short time ago I was returning to my hotel. It was a bitter cold night, the ground slippery, and no taxi to be had. Half a block behind me followed another man, evidently as anxious as myself to get under cover. Suddenly my legs went up in the air. In the same instant there was a flash in my brain, the nerves responded, the muscles contracted, I swung thru 180 degrees and landed on my hands. I resumed my walk as tho nothing had happened when the stranger caught up with me. "How old are you?" he asked, surveying me critically. "Oh, about fifty-nine," I replied. "What of it?" "Well," said he, "I have seen a cat do this but never a man." About a month since I wanted to order new eyeglasses and went to an oculist who put me thru the usual tests. He lookt at me increduously as I read off with ease the smallest print at considerable distance. But when I told him that I was past sixty he gasped in astonishment. Friends of mine often remark that my suits fit me like gloves but they do not know that all my clothing is made to measurements which were taken nearly 35 years ago and never changed. During this same period my weight has not varied one pound.

In this connection I may tell a funny story. One evening, in the winter of 1885, Mr. Edison, Edward H. Johnson, the President of the Edison Illuminating Company, Mr. Batchellor, Manager of the works, and myself entered a little place opposite 65 Fifth Avenue where the offices of the company were located. Someone suggested guessing weights and I was induced to step on a scale. Edison felt me all over and said: "Tesla weighs 152 lbs. to an ounce," and he guest it exactly. Stript I weighed 142 lbs. and that is still my weight. I whispered to Mr. Johnson: "How is it possible that Edison could guess my weight so closely?" "Well," he said, lowering his voice, "I will tell you, confidentially, but you must not say anything. He was employed for a long time in a Chicago slaughter-house where he weighed thousands of hogs every day! That's why." My friend, the Hon. Chauncey M. Depew, tells of an Englishman on whom he sprung one of his original anecdotes and who listened with a puzzled expression but — a year later — laughed out loud. I will frankly confess it took me longer than that to appreciate Johnson's joke.

Now, my well being is simply the result of a careful and measured mode of living and perhaps the most astonishing

thing is that three times in my youth I was rendered by illness a
hopeless physical wreck and given up by physicians. More
than this, thru ignorance and lightheartedness, I got into all
sorts of difficulties, dangers and scrapes from which I extri-
cated myself as by enchantment. I was almost drowned a dozen
times; was nearly boiled alive and just mist being cremated. I
was entombed, lost and frozen. I had hair-breadth escapes
from mad dogs, hogs, and other wild animals. I past thru
dreadful diseases and met with all kinds of odd mishaps and
that I am hale and hearty today seems like a miracle. But as I
recall these incidents to my mind I feel convinced that my
preservation was not altogether accidental.

An inventor's endeavor is essentially lifesaving. Whether
he harnesses forces, improves devices, or provides new com-
forts and conveniences, he is adding to the safety of our existence. He is also better qualified than the average individual to
protect himself in peril, for he is observant and resourceful. If I
had no other evidence that I was, in a measure, possest of such
qualities I would find it in these personal experiences. The
reader will be able to judge for himself if I mention one or two
instances. On one occasion, when about 14 years old, I wanted
to scare some friends who were bathing with me. My plan was
to dive under a long floating structure and slip out quietly at
the other end. Swimming and diving came to me as naturally
as to a duck and I was confident that I could perform the feat.
Accordingly I plunged into the water and, when out of view,
turned around and proceeded rapidly towards the opposite
side. Thinking that I was safely beyond the structure, I rose to
the surface but to my dismay struck a beam. Of course, I
quickly dived and forged ahead with rapid strokes until my
breath was beginning to give out. Rising for the second time,
my head came again in contact with a beam. Now I was
becoming desperate. However, summoning all my energy, I
made a third frantic attempt but the result was the same. The
torture of supprest breathing was getting unendurable, my
brain was reeling and I felt myself sinking. At that moment,
when my situation seemed absolutely hopeless, I experienced
one of those flashes of light and the structure above me

appeared before my vision. I either discerned or guest that there was a little space between the surface of the water and the boards resting on the beams and, with consciousness nearly gone, I floated up, prest my mouth close to the planks and managed to inhale a little air, unfortunately mingled with a spray of water which nearly choked me. Several times I repeated this procedure as in a dream until my heart, which was racing at a terrible rate, quieted down and I gained composure. After that I made a number of unsuccessful dives, having completely lost the sense of direction, but finally succeeded in getting out of the trap when my friends had already given me up and were fishing for my body.

That bathing season was spoiled for me thru recklessness but I soon forgot the lesson and only two years later I fell into a worse predicament. There was a large flour mill with a dam across the river near the city where I was studying at that time. As a rule the height of the water was only two or three inches above the dam and to swim out to it was a sport not very dangerous in which I often indulged. One day I went alone to the river to enjoy myself as usual. When I was a short distance from the masonry, however, I was horrified to observe that the water had risen and was carrying me along swiftly. I tried to get away but it was too late. Luckily, tho, I saved myself from being swept over by taking hold of the wall with both hands. The pressure against my chest was great and I was barely able to keep my head above the surface. Not a soul was in sight and my voice was lost in the roar of the fall. Slowly and gradually I became exhausted and unable to withstand the strain longer. Just as I was about to let go, to be dashed against the rocks below, I saw in a flash of light a familiar diagram illustrating the hydraulic principle that the pressure of a fluid in motion is proportionate to the area exposed, and automatically I turned on my left side. As if by magic the pressure was reduced and I found it comparatively easy in that position to resist the force of the stream. But the danger still confronted me. I knew that sooner or later I would be carried down, as it was not possible for any help to reach me in time, even if I attracted attention. I am ambidextrous now but then I was lefthanded and had comparatively little strength in my right arm. For this reason I did not dare to turn on the other side to rest and nothing remained but to slowly push my body along the dam. I had to get away from the mill towards which my face was turned as the current there was much swifter and deeper. It was a long and painful ordeal and I came near to failing at its very end for I was confronted with a depression in the masonry. I managed to get over with the last ounce of my force and fell in a swoon when I reached the bank, where I was found. I had torn virtually all the skin from my left side and it took several weeks before the fever subsided and I was well. These are only two of many instances but they may be sufficient to show that had it not been for the inventor's instinct I would not have lived to tell this tale.

Interested people have often asked me how and when I began to invent. This I can only answer from my present recollection in the light of which the first attempt I recall was rather ambitious for it involved the invention of an *apparatus* and a *method*. In the former I was anticipated but the latter was original. It happened in this way. One of my playmates had come into the possession of a hook and fishing-tackle which created quite an excitement in the village, and the next morning all started out to catch frogs. I was left alone and deserted owing to a quarrel with this boy. I had never seen a real hook and pictured it as something wonderful, endowed with peculiar qualities, and was despairing not to be one of the party. Urged by necessity, I somehow got hold of a piece of soft iron wire, hammered the end to a sharp point between two stones, bent it into shape, and fastened it to a strong string. I then cut a rod, gathered some bait, and went down to the brook where there were frogs in abundance. But I could not catch any and was almost discouraged when it occurred to me to dangle the empty hook in front of a frog sitting on a stump. At first he collapsed but by and by his eyes bulged out and became bloodshot, he swelled to twice his normal size and made a vicious snap at the hook. Immediately I pulled him up. I tried the same thing again and again and the method proved infallible. When my comrades, who in spite of their fine outfit had caught nothing, came to me they were green with envy. For a long time I kept my secret and enjoyed the monopoly but finally yielded to the spirit of Christmas. Every boy could then do the same and the following summer brought disaster to the frogs.

In my next attempt I seem to have acted under the first instinctive impulse which later dominated me — to harness the energies of nature to the service of man. I did this thru the medium of May-bugs — or June-bugs as they are called in America — which were a veritable pest in that country and sometimes broke the branches of trees by the sheer weight of their bodies. The bushes were black with them. I would attach as many as four of them to a crosspiece, rotably arranged on a thin spindle, and transmit the motion of the same to a large disc and so derive considerable "power." These creatures were remarkably efficient, for once they were started they had no sense to stop and continued whirling for hours and hours and the hotter it was the harder they worked. All went well until a strange boy came to the place. He was the son of a retired officer in the Austrian Army. That urchin ate May-bugs alive and enjoyed them as tho they were the finest blue-point oysters. That disgusting sight terminated my endeavors in this promising field and I have never since been able to touch a May-bug or any other insect for that matter.

After that, I believe, I undertook to take apart and assemble the clocks of my grandfather. In the former operation I was always successful but often failed in the latter. So it came that he brought my work to a sudden halt in a manner not too delicate and it took thirty years before I tackled another clockwork again. Shortly thereafter I went into the manufacture of a kind of pop-gun which comprised a hollow tube, a piston, and two plugs of hemp. When firing the gun, the piston was prest against the stomach and the tube was pushed back quickly with both hands. The air between the plugs was comprest and raised to high temperature and one of them was expelled with a loud report. The art consisted in selecting a tube of the proper taper from the hollow stalks which were [*here a line of type was dropped in the original — Ed.*] did very well with that gun but my activities interfered with the window panes in our house and met with painful discouragement. If I remember rightly, I then took to carving swords from pieces of furniture which I could conveniently obtain. At that time I was under the sway of the Serbian national poetry and full of admiration for the feats of the heroes. I used to spend hours in mowing down my enemies in the form of corn-stalks which ruined the crops and netted me several spankings from my mother. Moreover these were not of the formal kind but the genuine article.

I had all this and more behind me before I was six years old and had past thru one year of elementary school in the village of Smiljan where I was born. At this juncture we moved to the little city of Gospić nearby. This change of residence was like a calamity to me. It almost broke my heart to part from our pigeons, chickens and sheep, and our magnificent flock of geese which used to rise to the clouds in the morning and return from the feeding grounds at sundown in battle formation, so perfect that it would have put a squadron of the best aviators of the present day to shame. In our new house I was but a prisoner, watching the strange people I saw thru the

The Tesla family residence in Gospić. The "Real Gymnasium" where he studied is partially visible in the foreground. The man in flowing robes on the right is Tesla's uncle Petar, Serbian Orthodox Bishop of Bosnia.

window blinds. My bashfulness was such that I would rather have faced a roaring lion than one of the city dudes who strolled about. But my hardest trial came on Sunday when I had to dress up and attend the service. There I met with an accident, the mere thought of which made my blood curdle like sour milk for years afterwards. It was my second adventure in a church. Not long before I was entombed for a night in an old chapel on an inaccessible mountain which was visited only once a year. It was an awful experience, but this one was worse. There was a wealthy lady in town, a good but pompous woman, who used to come to the church gorgeously painted up and attired with an enormous train and attendants. One Sunday I had just finished ringing the bell in the belfry and rushed downstairs when this grand dame was sweeping out and I jumped on her train. It tore off with a ripping noise which sounded like a salvo of musketry fired by raw recruits. My father was livid with rage. He gave me a gentle slap on the cheek, the only corporal punishment he ever administered to me but I almost feel it now. The embarrassment and confusion that followed are indescribable. I was practically ostracised until something else happened which redeemed me in the estimation of the community.

An enterprising young merchant had organized a fire department. A new fire engine was purchased, uniforms provided and the men drilled for service and parade. The engine was, in reality, a pump to be worked by sixteen men and was beautifully painted red and black. One afternoon the official trial was prepared for and the machine was transported to the river. The entire population turned out to witness the great spectacle. When all the speeches and ceremonies were concluded, the command was given to pump, but not a drop of water came from the nozzle. The professors and experts tried in vain to locate the trouble. The fizzle was complete when I arrived at the scene. My knowledge of the mechanism was nil and I knew next to nothing of air pressure, but instinctively I felt for the suction hose in the water and found that it had collapsed. When I waded in the river and opened it up the water rushed forth and not a few Sunday clothes were spoiled.

Archimedes running naked thru the streets of Syracuse and shouting Eureka at the top of his voice did not make a greater impression than myself. I was carried on the shoulders and was the hero of the day.

Upon settling in the city I began a four-years' course in the so-called Normal School preparatory to my studies at the College or *Real Gymnasium*. During this period my boyish efforts and exploits, as well as troubles, continued. Among other things I attained the unique distinction of champion crow catcher in the country. My method of procedure was extremely simple. I would go in the forest, hide in the bushes, and imitate the call of the bird. Usually I would get several answers and in a short while a crow would flutter down into the shrubbery near me. After that all I needed to do was to throw a piece of cardboard to distract its attention, jump up and grab it before it could extricate itself from the under-growth. In this way I would capture as many as I desired. But on one occasion something occurred which made me respect them. I had caught a fine pair of birds and was returning home with a friend. When we left the forest, thousands of crows had gathered making a frightful racket. In a few minutes they rose in pursuit and soon enveloped us. The fun lasted until all of a sudden I received a blow on the back of my head which knocked me down. Then they attacked me viciously. I was compelled to release the two birds and was glad to join my friend who had taken refuge in a cave.

In the schoolroom there were a few mechanical models which interested me and turned my attention to water tur-bines. I constructed many of these and found great pleasure in operating them. How extraordinary was my life an incident may illustrate. My uncle had no use for this kind of pastime and more than once rebuked me. I was fascinated by a description of Niagara Falls I had perused, and pictured in my imagination a big wheel run by the Falls. I told my uncle that I would go to America and carry out this scheme. Thirty years later I saw my ideas carried out at Niagara and marveled at the unfathomable mystery of the mind.

I made all kinds of other contrivances and contraptions

but among these the arbalists I produced were the best. My arrows, when shot, disappeared from sight and at close range traversed a plank of pine one inch thick. Thru the continuous tightening of the bows I developed skin on my stomach very much like that of a crocodile and I am often wondering whether it is due to this exercise that I am able even now to digest cobble-stones! Nor can I pass in silence my performances with the sling which would have enabled me to give a stunning exhibit at the Hippodrome. And now I will tell of one of my feats with this antique implement of war which will strain to the utmost the credulity of the reader. I was practicing while walking with my uncle along the river. The sun was setting, the trout were playful and from time to time one would shoot up into the air, its glistening body sharply defined against a projecting rock beyond. Of course any boy might have hit a fish under these propitious conditions but I undertook a much more difficult task and I foretold to my uncle, to the minutest detail, what I intended doing. I was to hurl a stone to meet the fish, press its body against the rock, and cut it in two. It was no sooner said than done. My uncle looked at me almost scared out of his wits and exclaimed *"Vade retro Satanas!"* and it was a few days before he spoke to me again. Other records, however great, will be eclipsed but I feel that I could peacefully rest on my laurels for a thousand years.

Nikola Tesla at age 29, shortly after his arrival in the United States.

III. MY LATER ENDEAVORS

The Discovery of the Rotating Magnetic Field

A T the age of ten I entered the Real Gymnasium which was a new and fairly well equipt institution. In the department of physics were various models of classical scientific apparatus, electrical and mechanical. The demonstrations and experiments performed from time to time by the instructors fascinated me and were undoubtedly a powerful incentive to invention. I was also passionately fond of mathematical studies and often won the professor's praise for rapid calculation. This was due to my acquired facility of visualizing the figures and performing the operations, not in the usual intuitive manner, but as in actual life. Up to a certain degree of complexity it was absolutely the same to me whether I wrote the symbols on the board or conjured them before my mental vision. But freehand drawing, to which many hours of the course were devoted, was an annoyance I could not endure. This was rather remarkable as most of the members of the family excelled in it. Perhaps my aversion was simply due to the predilection I found in undisturbed thought. Had it not been for a few exceptionally stupid boys, who could not do anything at all, my record would have been the worst. It was a serious handicap as under the then existing educational regime, drawing being obligatory, this deficiency threatened to spoil my whole career and my father had considerable trouble in railroading me from one class to another.

In the second year at that institution I became obsest with

the idea of producing continuous motion thru steady air pressure. The pump incident, of which I have told, had set afire my youthful imagination and imprest me with the boundless possibilities of a vacuum. I grew frantic in my desire to harness this inexhaustible energy but for a long time I was groping in the dark. Finally, however, my endeavors crystallized in an invention which was to enable me to achieve what no other mortal ever attempted. Imagine a cylinder freely rotatable on two bearings and partly surrounded by a rectangular trough which fits it perfectly. The open side of the trough is closed by a partition so that the cylindrical segment within the enclosure divides the latter into two compartments entirely separated from each other by air-tight sliding joints. One of these compartments being sealed and once for all exhausted, the other remaining open, a perpetual rotation of the cylinder would result, at least, I thought so. A wooden model was constructed and fitted with infinite care and when I applied the pump on one side and actually observed that there was a tendency to turning, I was delirious with joy. Mechanical flight was the one thing I wanted to accomplish altho still under the discouraging recollection of a bad fall I sustained by jumping with an umbrella from the top of a building. Every day I used to transport myself thru the air to distant regions but could not understand just how I managed to do it. Now I had something concrete — a flying machine with nothing more than a rotating shaft, flapping wings, and — a vacuum of unlimited power! From that time on I made my daily aerial excursions in a vehicle of comfort and luxury as might have befitted King Solomon. It took years before I understood that the atmospheric pressure acted at right angles to the surface of the cylinder and that the slight rotary effort I observed was due to a leak. Tho this knowledge came gradually it gave me a painful shock.

I had hardly completed my course at the Real Gymnasium when I was prostrated with a dangerous illness or rather, a score of them, and my condition became so desperate that I was given up by physicians. During this period I was permitted to read constantly, obtaining books from the Public

Library which had been neglected and entrusted to me for classification of the works and preparation of the catalogues. One day I was handed a few volumes of new literature unlike anything I had ever read before and so captivating as to make me utterly forget my hopeless state. They were the earlier works of Mark Twain and to them might have been due the miraculous recovery which followed. Twenty-five years later, when I met Mr. Clemens and we formed a friendship between us, I told him of the experience and was amazed to see that great man of laughter burst into tears.

My studies were continued at the higher Real Gymnasium in Carlstadt, Croatia, where one of my aunts resided. She was a distinguished lady, the wife of a Colonel who was an old war-horse having participated in many battles. I never can forget the three years I past at their home. No fortress in time of war was under a more rigid discipline. I was fed like a canary bird. All the meals were of the highest quality and deliciously prepared but short in quantity by a thousand percent. The slices of ham cut by my aunt were like tissue paper. When the Colonel would put something substantial on my plate she would snatch it away and say excitedly to him: "Be careful, Niko is very delicate." I had a voracious appetite and suffered like Tantalus. But I lived in an atmosphere of refinement and artistic taste quite unusual for those times and conditions. The land was low and marshy and malaria fever never left me while there despite of the enormous amounts of quinin I consumed. Occasionally the river would rise and drive an army of rats into the buildings, devouring everything even to the bundles of the fierce paprika. These pests were to me a welcome diversion. I thinned their ranks by all sorts of means, which won me the unenviable distinction of rat-catcher in the community. At last, however, my course was completed, the misery ended, and I obtained the certificate of maturity which brought me to the cross-roads.

During all those years my parents never wavered in their resolve to make me embrace the clergy, the mere thought of which filled me with dread. I had become intensely interested in electricity under the stimulating influence of my Professor of Physics, who was an ingenious man and often demonstrated the principles by apparatus of his own invention. Among these I recall a device in the shape of a freely rotatable bulb, with tinfoil coatings, which was made to spin rapidly when connected to a static machine. It is impossible for me to convey an adequate idea of the intensity of feeling I experienced in witnessing his exhibitions of these mysterious phenomena. Every impression produced a thousand echoes in my mind. I wanted to know more of this wonderful force; I longed for experiment and investigation and resigned myself to the inevitable with aching heart.

Just as I was making ready for the long journey home I received word that my father wished me to go on a shooting expedition. It was a strange request as he had been always strenuously opposed to this kind of sport. But a few days later I learned that the cholera was raging in that district and, taking advantage of an opportunity, I returned to Gospić in disregard of my parents' wishes. It is incredible how absolutely ignorant people were as to the causes of this scourge which visited the country in intervals of from fifteen to twenty years. They thought that the deadly agents were transmitted thru the air and filled it with pungent odors and smoke. In the meantime they drank the infected water and died in heaps. I contracted the awful disease on the very day of my arrival and altho surviving the crisis, I was confined to bed for nine months with scarcely any ability to move. My energy was completely exhausted and for the second time I found myself at death's door. In one of the sinking spells which was thought to be the last, my father rushed into the room. I still see his pallid face as he tried to cheer me in tones belying his assurance. "Perhaps," I said, "I may get well if you will let me study engineering." "You will go to the best technical institution in the world," he solemnly replied, and I knew that he meant it. A heavy weight was lifted from my mind but the relief would have come too late had it not been for a marvelous cure brought about thru a bitter decoction of a peculiar bean. I came to life like another Lazarus to the utter amazement of everybody. My father insisted that I spend a year in healthful physical outdoor exercises to which I reluctantly consented. For most of this term I roamed in the mountains, loaded with a hunter's outfit and a bundle of books, and this contact with nature made me stronger in body as well as in mind. I thought and planned, and conceived many ideas almost as a rule delusive. The vision was clear enough but the knowledge of principles was very limited. In one of my inventions I proposed to convey letters and packages across the seas, thru a submarine tube, in spherical containers of sufficient strength to resist the hydraulic pressure. The pumping plant, intended to force the water thru the tube, was accurately figured and designed and all other particulars carefully worked out. Only one trifling detail, of no consequence, was lightly dismist. I assumed an arbitrary velocity of the water and, what is more, took pleasure in making it high, thus arriving at a stupendous performance supported by faultless calculations. Subsequent reflections, however, on the resistance of pipes to fluid flow determined me to make this invention public property.

Another one of my projects was to construct a ring around the equator which would, of course, float freely and could be arrested in its spinning motion by reactionary forces, thus enabling travel at a rate of about one thousand miles an hour, impracticable by rail. The reader will smile. The plan was difficult of execution, I will admit, but not nearly so bad as that of a well-known New York professor, who wanted to pump the air from the torrid to the temperate zones, entirely forgetful of the fact that the Lord had provided a gigantic machine for this very purpose.

Still another scheme, far more important and attractive, was to derive power from the rotational energy of terrestrial bodies. I had discovered that objects on the earth's surface, owing to the diurnal rotation of the globe, are carried by the same alternately in and against the direction of translatory movement. From this results a great change in momentum which could be utilized in the simplest imaginable manner to furnish motive effort in any habitable region of the world. I cannot find words to describe my disappointment when later I realized that I was in the predicament of Archimedes, who vainly sought for a fixt point in the universe.

At the termination of my vacation I was sent to the Polytechnic School in Gratz, Styria, which my father had chosen as one of the oldest and best reputed institutions. That was the moment I had eagerly awaited and I began my studies under good auspices and firmly resolved to succeed. My previous training was above the average, due to my father's teaching and opportunities afforded. I had acquired the knowledge of a number of languages and waded thru the books of several libraries, picking up information more or less useful. Then again, for the first time, I could choose my subjects as I liked, and free-hand drawing was to bother me no more. I had made up my mind to give my parents a surprise, and during the whole first year I regularly started my work at three o'clock in the morning and continued until eleven at night, no Sundays or holidays excepted. As most of my fellow-students took thinks easily, naturally enough I eclipsed all records. In the course of that year I past thru nine exams and the professors thought I deserved more than the highest qualifications. Armed with their flattering certificates, I went home for a short rest, expecting a triumph, and was mortified when my father made light of these hardwon honors. That almost killed my ambition; but later, after he had died, I was pained to find a package of letters which the professors had written him to the effect that unless he took me away from the Institution I would be killed thru overwork. Thereafter I devoted myself chiefly to physics, mechanics and mathematical studies, spending the hours of leisure in the libraries. I had a veritable mania for finishing whatever I began, which often got me into difficulties. On one occasion I started to read the works of Voltaire when I learned, to my dismay, that there were close on one hundred large volumes in small print which that monster had written while drinking seventy-two cups of black coffee per diem. It had to be done, but when I laid aside the last book I was very glad, and said, "Never more!"

My first year's showing had won me the appreciation and friendship of several professors. Among these were Prof. Rogner, who was teaching arithmetical subjects and geome-

try; Prof. Poeschl, who held the chair of theoretical and experimental physics, and Dr. Allé, who taught integral calculus
and specialized in differential equations. This scientist was the
most brilliant lecturer to whom I ever listened. He took a
special interest in my progress and would frequently remain
for an hour or two in the lecture room, giving me problems to
solve, in which I delighted. To him I explained a flying
machine I had conceived, not an illusionary invention, but
one based on sound, scientific principles, which has become
realizable thru my turbine and will soon be given to the world.
Both Professors Rogner and Poeschl were curious men. The
former had peculiar ways of expressing himself and whenever
he did so there was a riot, followed by a long and embarrassing
pause. Prof. Poeschl was a methodical and thoroly grounded
German. He had enormous feet and hands like the paws of a
bear, but all of his experiments were skillfully performed with
clock-like precision and without a miss.

It was in the second year of my studies that we received a
Gramme dynamo from Paris, having the horseshoe form of a
laminated field magnet, and a wire-wound armature with a
commutator. It was connected up and various effects of the
currents were shown. While Prof. Poeschl was making demonstrations, running the machine as a motor, the brushes gave
trouble, sparking badly, and I observed that it might be possible to operate a motor without these appliances. But he
declared that it could not be done and did me the honor of
delivering a lecture on the subject, at the conclusion of which
he remarked: "Mr. Tesla may accomplish great things, but he
certainly never will do this. It would be equivalent to converting a steadily pulling force, like that of gravity, into a rotary
effort. It is a perpetual motion scheme, an impossible idea."
But instinct is something which transcends knowledge. We
have, undoubtedly, certain finer fibers that enable us to per-
ceive truths when logical deduction, or any other willful effort
of the brain, is futile. For a time I wavered, imprest by the
professor's authority, but soon became convinced I was right
and undertook the task with all the fire and boundless confidence of youth.

One of Tesla's original polyphase induction motors, first demonstrated before the American Institute of Electrical Engineers in 1888. The rotating magnetic field created in this motor by out-of-phase alternating currents in the stationary coils pulls the rotor around by inducing secondary currents to flow within the rotor: the secondary magnetic field created by these rotor currents causes the rotor to race in pursuit of the rotating primary magnetic field — almost, but never quite, catching up. This motor is the most trouble-free in existence: its rotor, devoid of spark-creating brushes, slip-rings, and other electrical connections, is the motor's sole moving part, so that only the rotor bearings can ever wear out.

I started by first picturing in my mind a direct-current machine, running it and following the changing flow of the currents in the armature. Then I would imagine an alternator and investigate the processes taking place in a similar manner. Next I would visualize systems comprising motors and generators and operate them in various ways. The images I saw were to me perfectly real and tangible. All my remaining term in Gratz was passed in intense but fruitless efforts of this kind, and I almost came to the conclusion that the problem was insolvable. In 1880 I went to Prague, Bohemia, carrying out my father's wish to complete my education at the University there. It was in that city that I made a decided advance, which consisted in detaching the commutator from the machine and studying the phenomena in this new aspect, but still without result. In the year following there was a sudden change in my views of life. I realized that my parents had been making too great sacrifices on my account and resolved to relieve them of the burden. The wave of the American telephone had just reached the European continent and the system was to be installed in Budapest, Hungary. It appeared an ideal opportunity, all the more as a friend of our family was at the head of the enterprise. It was here that I suffered the complete breakdown of the nerves to which I have referred. What I experienced during the period of that illness surpasses all belief. My sight and hearing were always extraordinary. I could clearly discern objects in the distance when others saw no trace of them. Several times in my boyhood I saved the houses of our neighbors from fire by hearing the faint crackling sounds which did not disturb their sleep, and calling for help.

In 1899, when I was past forty and carrying on my experiments in Colorado, I could hear very distinctly thunderclaps at a distance of 550 miles. The limit of audition for my young assistants was scarcely more than 150 miles. My ear was thus over thirteen times more sensitive. Yet at that time I was, so to speak, stone deaf in comparison with the acuteness of my hearing while under the nervous strain. In Budapest I could hear the ticking of a watch with three rooms between me and the time-piece. A fly alighting on a table in the room would cause a dull thud in my ear. A carriage passing at a distance of a few miles fairly shook my whole body. The whistle of a locomotive twenty or thirty miles away made the bench or chair on which I sat vibrate so strongly that the pain was unbearable. The ground under my feet trembled continuously. I had to support my bed on rubber cushions to get any rest at all. The roaring noises from near and far often produced the effect of spoken words which would have frightened me had I not been able to resolve them into their accidental components. The sun's rays, when periodically intercepted, would cause blows of such force on my brain that they would stun me. I had to summon all my will power to pass under a bridge or other structure as I experienced a crushing pressure on the skull. In the dark I had the sense of a bat and could detect the presence of an object at a distance of twelve feet by a peculiar creepy sensation on the forehead. My pulse varied from a few to two hundred and sixty beats and all the tissues of the body with twitchings and tremors which was perhaps the hardest to bear.* A renowned physician who gave me daily large doses of Bromid of Potassium pronounced my malady unique and incurable. It is my eternal regret that I was not under the observation of experts in physiology and psychology at that time. I clung desperately to life, but never expected to recover. Can anyone believe that so hopeless a physical wreck could ever be transformed into a man of astonishing strength and tenacity, able to work thirty-eight years almost without a day's interruption, and find himself still strong and fresh in body and mind? Such is my case. A powerful desire to live and to continue the work, and the assistance of a devoted friend and athlete accomplished the wonder. My health returned and with it the vigor of mind. In attacking the problem again I almost regretted that the struggle was soon to end. I had so much energy to spare. When I undertook the task it was not with a resolve such as men often make. With me it was a sacred vow, a question of life and death. I knew that I

---

*The verb between "body" and "with" was apparently omitted in the original.

would perish if I failed. Now I felt that the battle was won. Back in the deep recesses of the brain was the solution, but I could not yet give it outward expression. One afternoon, which is ever present in my recollection, I was enjoying a walk with my friend in the City Park and reciting poetry. At that age I knew entire books by heart, word for word. One of these was Göethe's "Faust." The sun was just setting and reminded me of the glorious passage:

> *"Sie rückt und weicht, der Tag ist überlebt,*
> *Dort eilt sie hin und fördert neues Leben.*
> *Oh, dass kein Flügel mich vom Boden hebt*
> *Ihr nach und immer nach zu streben!**
> * * *
> *Ein schöner Traum indessen sie entweicht,*
> *Ach, zu des Geistes Flügeln wird so leicht*
> *Kein körperlicher Flügel sich gesellen!"§*

As I uttered these inspiring words the idea came like a flash of lightning and in an instant the truth was revealed. I drew with a stick on the sand the diagrams shown six years later in my address before the American Institute of Electrical Engineers, and my companion understood them perfectly. The images I saw were wonderfully sharp and clear and had the solidity of metal and stone, so much so that I told him: "See my motor here; watch me reverse it." I cannot begin to describe my emotions. Pygmalion seeing his statue come to life could not have been more deeply moved. A thousand secrets of nature which I might have stumbled upon accidentally I would have given for that one which I had wrested from her against all odds and at the peril of my existence.

---

*"The glow retreats, done is the day of toil;
It yonder hastes, new fields of life exploring;
Ah, that no wing can lift me from the soil
Upon its track to follow, follow soaring!"

§A glorious dream! though now the glories fade.
Alas! the wings that lift the mind no aid
Of wings to lift the body can bequeath me."

HYDRAULIC ANALOG OF TESLA TWO PHASE INDUCTION MOTOR

CURRENT I   CURRENT II

Revoluble Disc in Water Chamber

Blade fixed on disc

CURVES SHOWING CYCLE OF OPERATIONS

"Phase" difference of 90° between current maximums.

CURRENT I MAX. +
CURRENT II MAX. +
CURRENT I
CURRENT II
CURRENT I MAX. –
CURRENT II MAX. –

POSITIVE FLOW
ZERO FLOW
NEGATIVE OR REVERSE FLOW

MOTOR SCHEMATICS SHOWING MAGNETIC FIELD ROTATION

ROTOR

CURRENT II
CURRENT I

(circuit wiring is omitted after first schematic)

HOW POLYPHASE CURRENTS CREATE THE ROTATING MAGNETIC FIELD.

Editor's note: This illustration has been altered to eliminate contradictions in the original. The original is reproduced on page 111.

This analog is designed to help readers conceptualize how polyphase alternating currents can create a rotating magnetic field. Today's polyphase systems use three currents of different phase, but Tesla at first used *two* alternating currents, each confined to a separate two-wire circuit. These currents are identical but 90° out-of-phase, which simply means that they are staggered so that the peak output points of each coincide with the 'dead points' of the other. (An alternating current momentarily ceases to flow each time it reverses its direction of flow; the 60-cycle-per-second current commonly used in North America has 120 of these 'dead' or reversal points every second.) The hydraulic motor at the top of the illustration shows an analogous 90° phase separation between two *fluid* alternating currents wherein one pair of piston pumps is at mid-stroke whenever the other pair has reached its limits of travel: one or the other current is always moving and producing power. This phase relationship is permanently fixed by the arrangement of the crankshaft cranks at right angles to one another.

The phase separation between polyphase *electric* currents is similarly predetermined: each current phase is produced within the polyphase generator by a pair of coils mounted at fixed angles to the pairs that produce other phases. Such a generator is not illustrated here, but its construction is duplicated in a polyphase *motor*. In the two-phase motor shown, two pairs of coils, each pair connected to a different current phase, are set at right angles to one another. These paired coils act as electromagnets whose magnetic polarity reverses whenever the alter-nating current which energizes them reverses its direction of flow. Thus it can be seen that when current I is at a positive maximum, its coils produce a strong magnetic field with the 'north-south' polar orientation shown in the diagram at *1*. When current I has fallen to zero, demagnetizing its coils (2), current II has just reached *its* maximum value, producing a new field with the polar orientation shown. Then this current falls to zero, demagnetizing its coils, just when current I has reversed its direction and reached its *opposite* maximum value (3), producing a magnetic field whose polarity is opposite that earlier produced in the same coils. Finally, current I again falls to zero and current II reverses in *its* turn (4) — the reader can see that there are no dead spots, and that the magnetic poles created shift progressively around the motor. Most important of all, this shifting of the poles is perfectly smooth and continuous, as if an actual magnet were whirling about the motor's periphery. This is because the magnetic fields of the two currents *merge* whenever both currents are at partial power, as the intermediate illustrations show. As one field loses and the next gains strength the *resultant* field never weakens — the sum of the two fields always equals the strength of a single field at full power — but it invisibly moves through space, describing a perfect circle as the relative contributions of the two constantly varying currents change. Readers familiar with simple harmonic motion will recognize the analogy with a pendulum in circular motion: that motion is simply the sum of two matching oscillations, at right angles to one another and 90° out-of-phase.

Nikola Tesla, aged 39, at the height of his fame.

IV. THE DISCOVERY OF
THE TESLA COIL
AND TRANSFORMER

FOR a while I gave myself up entirely to the intense enjoyment of picturing machines and devising new forms. It was a mental state of happiness about as complete as I have ever known in life. Ideas came in an uninterrupted stream and the only difficulty I had was to hold them fast. The pieces of apparatus I conceived were to me absolutely real and tangible in every detail, even to the minutest marks and signs of wear. I delighted in imagining the motors constantly running, for in this way they presented to the mind's eye a more fascinating sight. When natural inclination develops into a passionate desire, one advances towards his goal in seven-league boots. In less than two months I evolved virtually all the types of motors and modifications of the system which are now identified with my name. It was, perhaps, providential that the necessities of existence commanded a temporary halt to this consuming activity of the mind. I came to Budapest prompted by a premature report concerning the telephone enterprise and, as irony of fate willed it, I had to accept a position as draftsman in the Central Telegraph Office of the Hungarian Government at a salary which I deem it my privilege not to disclose! Fortunately, I soon won the interest of the Inspector-in-Chief and was thereafter employed on calculations, designs and estimates in connection with new installations, until the Telephone Exchange was started, when I took charge of the same. The knowledge and practical experience I gained in the course of this work was most valuable and the employment gave me ample opportunities for the exercise of my inventive faculties. I made several improvements in the Central Station apparatus and perfected a telephone repeater or amplifier which was never patented or publicly described but would be creditable to me even today. In recognition of my efficient assistance the organizer of the undertaking, Mr. Puskas, upon disposing of his business in Budapest, offered me a position in Paris which I gladly accepted.

I never can forget the deep impression that magic city produced on my mind. For several days after my arrival I roamed thru the streets in utter bewilderment of the new spectacle. The attractions were many and irresistible, but, alas, the income was spent as soon as received. When Mr. Puskas asked me how I was getting along in the new sphere, I described the situation accurately in the statement that "the last twenty-nine days of the month are the toughest!" I led a rather strenuous life in what would now be termed "Rooseveltian fashion." Every morning, regardless of weather, I would go from the Boulevard St. Marcel, where I resided, to a bathing house on the Seine, plunge into the water, loop the circuit twenty-seven times and then walk an hour to reach Ivry, where the Company's factory was located. There I would have a woodchopper's breakfast at half-past seven o'clock and then eagerly await the lunch hour, in the meanwhile cracking hard nuts for the Manager of the Works, Mr. Charles Batchellor, who was an intimate friend and assistant of Edison. Here I was thrown in contact with a few Americans who fairly fell in love with me because of my proficiency in—billiards. To these men I explained my invention and one of them, Mr. D. Cunningham, Foreman of the Mechanical Department, offered to form a stock company. The proposal seemed to me comical in the extreme. I did not have the faintest conception of what that meant except that it was an American way of doing things. Nothing came of it, however, and during the next few months I had to travel from one to another place in France and Germany to cure the ills of the power plants. On my return to

Paris I submitted to one of the administrators of the Company, Mr. Rau, a plan for improving their dynamos and was given an opportunity. My success was complete and the delighted directors accorded me the privilege of developing automatic regulators which were much desired. Shortly after there was some trouble with the lighting plant which had been installed at the new railroad station in Strassburg, Alsace. The wiring was defective and on the occasion of the opening ceremonies a large part of a wall was blown out thru a short-circuit right in the presence of old Emperor William I. The German Government refused to take the plant and the French Company was facing a serious loss. On account of my knowledge of the German language and past experience, I was entrusted with the difficult task of straightening out matters and early in 1883 I went to Strassburg on that mission.

Some of the incidents in that city have left an indelible record on my memory. By a curious coincidence, a number of men who subsequently achieved fame, lived there about that time. In later life I used to say, "There were bacteria of greatness in that old town. Others caught the disease but I escaped!" The practical work, correspondence, and conferences with officials kept me preoccupied day and night, but as soon as I was able to manage I undertook the construction of a simple motor in a mechanical shop opposite the railroad station, having brought with me from Paris some material for that purpose. The consummation of the experiment was, however, delayed until the summer of that year when I finally had the satisfaction of *seeing rotation effected by alternating currents of different phase, and without sliding contacts or commutator,* as I had conceived a year before. It was an exquisite pleasure but not to compare with the delirium of joy following the first revelation.

Among my new friends was the former Mayor of the city, Mr. Bauzin, whom I had already in a measure acquainted with this and other inventions of mine and whose support I endeavored to enlist. He was sincerely devoted to me and put my project before several wealthy persons but, to my mortification, found no response. He wanted to help me in every possible way and the approach of the first of July, 1919, happens to remind me of a form of "assistance" I received from that charming man, which was not financial but none the less appreciated. In 1870, when the Germans invaded the country, Mr. Bauzin had buried a good sized allotment of St. Estèphe of 1801 and he came to the conclusion that he knew no worthier person than myself to consume that precious beverage. This, I may say, is one of the unforgettable incidents to which I have referred. My friend urged me to return to Paris as soon as possible and seek support there. This I was anxious to do but my work and negotiations were protracted owing to all sorts of petty obstacles I encountered so that at times the situation seemed hopeless.

Just to give an idea of German thoroness and "efficiency," I may mention here a rather funny experience. An incandescent lamp of 16 c.p. was to be placed in a hallway and upon selecting the proper location I ordered the *monteur* to run the wires. After working for a while he concluded that the engineer had to be consulted and this was done. The latter made several objections but ultimately agreed that the lamp should be placed two inches from the spot I had assigned, whereupon the work proceeded. Then the engineer became worried and told me that Inspector Averdeck should be notified. That important person called, investigated, debated, and decided that the lamp should be shifted back two inches, which was the place I had marked. It was not long, however, before Averdeck got cold feet himself and advised me that he had informed *Ober-Inspector* Hieronimus of the matter and that I should await his decision. It was several days before the *Ober-Inspector* was able to free himself of other pressing duties but at last he arrived and a two-hour debate followed, when he decided to move the lamp two inches farther. My hopes that this was the final act were shattered when the *Ober-Inspector* returned and said to me: *"Regierungsrath* Funke is so particular that I would not dare to give an order for placing this lamp without his explicit approval." Accordingly arrangements for a visit from that great man were made. We started cleaning up and polishing early in the morning. Everybody brushed up, I put on my gloves and when Funke came

The Tesla oscillation transformer (Tesla Coil) presented by Lord Kelvin before the British Association in August, 1897. This small and compact instrument, only 8 inches high, developed two square feet of streamers using 25 watts of power from the 110 volt direct current supply circuit. It consisted of a Tesla primary and secondary, condenser, and circuit controller. (See page 73.)

with his retinue he was ceremoniously received. After two hours' deliberation he suddenly exclaimed: "I must be going," and pointing to a place on the ceiling, he ordered me to put the lamp there. It was the exact spot which I had originally chosen,

So it went day after day with variations, but I was determined to achieve at whatever cost and in the end my efforts were rewarded. By the spring of 1884 all the differences were adjusted, the plant formally accepted, and I returned to Paris with pleasing anticipations. One of the administrators had promised me a liberal compensation in case I succeeded, as well as a fair consideration of the improvements I had made in their dynamos and I hoped to realize a substantial sum. There were three administrators whom I shall designate as A,B and C for convenience. When I called on A *he* told me that B had the say. This gentleman thought that only C could decide and the latter was quite sure that A alone had the power to act. After several laps of this *circulus viciosus,* it dawned upon me that my reward was a castle in Spain. The utter failure of my attempts to raise capital for development was another disappointment and when Mr. Batchellor prest me to go to America with a view of redesigning the Edison machines, I determined to try my fortunes in the Land of Golden Promise. But the chance was nearly mist. I liquefied my modest assets, secured accommodations and found myself at the railroad station as the train was pulling out. At that moment I discovered that my money and tickets were gone. What to do was the question. Hercules had plenty of time to deliberate but I had to decide while running alongside the train with opposite feelings surging in my brain like condenser oscillations. Resolve, helped by dexterity, won out in the nick of time and upon passing thru the usual experiences, as trivial as unpleasant, I managed to embark for New York with the remnants of my belongings, some poems and articles I had written, and a package of calculations relating to solutions of an unsolvable integral and to my flying machine. During the voyage I sat most of the time at the stern of the ship watching for an opportunity to save somebody from a watery grave, without the slightest thought of danger. Later when I had absorbed some of the practical American sense I shivered at the recollection and marvelled at my former folly.

I wish that I could put in words my first impressions of this country. In the Arabian Tales I read how genii transported people into a land of dreams to live thru delightful adventures. My case was just the reverse. The genii had carried me from a world of dreams into one of realities. What I had left was beautiful, artistic and fascinating in every way; what I saw here was machined, rough and unattractive. A burly policeman was twirling his stick which looked to me as big as a log. I approached him politely with the request to direct me. "Six blocks down, then to the left," he said, with murder in his eyes. "Is this America?" I asked myself in painful surprise. "It is a century behind Europe in civilization." When I went abroad in 1889 — five years having elapsed since my arrival here — I became convinced that *it was more than one hundred years AHEAD of Europe* and nothing has happened to this day to change my opinion.

The meeting with Edison was a memorable event in my life. I was amazed at this wonderful man who, without early advantages and scientific training, had accomplished so much. I had studied a dozen languages, delved in literature and art, and had spent my best years in libraries reading all sorts of stuff that fell into my hands, from Newton's *"Principia"* to the novels of Paul de Kock, and felt that most of my life had been squandered. But it did not take long before I recognized that it was the best thing I could have done. Within a few weeks I had won Edison's confidence and it came about in this way.

The S.S. *Oregon,* the fastest passenger steamer at that time, had both of its lighting machines disabled and its sailing was delayed. As the superstructure had been built after their installation it was impossible to remove them from the hold. The predicament was a serious one and Edison was much annoyed. In the evening I took the necessary instruments with me and went aboard the vessel where I stayed for the night. The dynamos were in bad condition, having several short-circuits and breaks, but with the assistance of the crew I succeeded in putting them in good shape. At five o'clock in the morning, when passing along Fifth Avenue on my way to the shop, I met Edison with Batchellor and a few others as they were returning home to retire. "Here is our Parisian running around at night," he said. When I told him that I was coming from the *Oregon* and had repaired both machines, he looked at me in silence and walked away without another word. But when he had gone some distance I heard him remark: "Batchellor, this is a d—n good man," and from that time on I had full freedom in directing the work. For nearly a year my regular hours were from 10.30 A.M. until 5 o'clock the next morning without a day's exception. Edison said to me: "I have had many hard-working assistants but you take the cake." During this period I designed twenty-four different types of standard machines with short cores and of uniform pattern which replaced the old ones. The Manager had promised me fifty thousand dollars on the completion of this task but it turned out to be a practical joke. This gave me a painful shock and I resigned my position.

Immediately thereafter some people approached me with the proposal of forming an arc light company under my name, to which I agreed. Here finally was an opportunity to develop the motor, but when I broached the subject to my new associates they said: "No, we want the arc lamp. We don't care for this alternating current of yours." In 1886 my system of arc lighting was perfected and adopted for factory and municipal lighting, and I was free, but with no other possession than a beautifully engraved certificate of stock of hypothetical value. Then followed a period of struggle in the new medium for which I was not fitted, but the reward came in the end and in April, 1887, the Tesla Electric Company was organized, providing a laboratory and facilities. The motors I built there were exactly as I had imagined them. I made no attempt to improve the design, but merely reproduced the pictures as they appeared to my vision and the operation was always as I expected.

In the early part of 1888 an arrangement was made with

the Westinghouse Company for the manufacture of the motors on a large scale. But great difficulties had still to be overcome. My system was based on the use of low frequency currents and the Westinghouse experts had adopted 133 cycles with the object of securing advantages in the transformation. They did not want to depart from their standard forms of apparatus and my efforts had to be concentrated upon adapting the motor to these conditions. Another necessity was to produce a motor capable of running efficiently at this frequency on two wires which was not easy of accomplishment.

At the close of 1889, however, my services in Pittsburg being no longer essential, I returned to New York and resumed experimental work in a laboratory on Grand Street, where I began immediately the design of high frequency machines. The problems of construction in this unexplored field were novel and quite peculiar and I encountered many difficulties. I rejected the inductor type, fearing that it might not yield perfect sine waves which were so important to resonant action. Had it not been for this I could have saved myself a great deal of labor. Another discouraging feature of the high frequency alternator seemed to be the inconstancy of speed which threatened to impose serious limitations to its use. I had already noted in my demonstrations before the American Institution of Electrical Engineers that several times the tune was lost, necessitating readjustment, and did not yet foresee, what I discovered long afterwards, a means of operating a machine of this kind at a speed constant to such a degree as not to vary more than a small fraction of one revolution between the extremes of load.

From many other considerations it appeared desirable to invent a simpler device for the production of electric oscillations. In 1856 Lord Kelvin had exposed the theory of the condenser discharge, but no practical application of that important knowledge was made. I saw the possibilities and undertook the development of induction apparatus on this principle. My progress was so rapid as to enable me to exhibit at my lecture in 1891 a coil giving sparks of *five inches*. On that occasion I frankly told the engineers of a defect involved in the

An illustration of spark discharges produced at Tesla's Colorado Springs wireless plant in 1899. The ball is 80 centimeters (31½ inches) in diameter, and is connected to the free end of a grounded resonant circuit 17 meters (55¾ feet) in diameter. Tesla calculated the disruptive potential of the ball at approximately 3 million volts. (V=75,000 x radius in cm.) The gigantic coil which produced these discharges had a primary 51 feet in diameter, and was capable of furnishing an 1100 ampere current in the high tension secondary.

transformation by the new method, namely, the loss in the spark gap. Subsequent investigation showed that no matter what medium is employed, be it air, hydrogen, mercury vapor, oil or a stream of electrons, the efficiency is the same. It is a law very much like that governing the conversion of mechanical energy. We may drop a weight from a certain height vertically down or carry it to the lower level along any devious path, it is immaterial insofar as the amount of work is concerned. Fortunately however, this drawback is not fatal as by proper proportioning of the resonant circuits an *efficiency of 85 per cent* is attainable. Since my early announcement of the invention it has come into universal use and wrought a revolution in many departments. But a still greater future awaits it. When in 1900 I obtained powerful discharges of 100 feet and flashed a current around the globe, I was reminded of the first tiny spark I observed in my Grand Street laboratory and was thrilled by sensations akin to those I felt when I discovered the *rotating magnetic field.*

Schematic of circuit connections in the oscillation transformer (Tesla coil) shown on page 69. The secondary circuit which slips into the primary is omitted.

MECHANICAL ANALOG FOR THE TESLA COIL

The revolutionary Tesla coil, now in universal use, was exhibited and explained by Tesla for the first time in his lecture before the American Institute of Electrical Engineers May 20, 1891. It has made possible the generation of automatically damped or undamped oscillations of any desired frequency and of perfectly constant period. The underlying principle may be briefly stated as follows: A source of electricity is made to charge a condenser and when the difference of potential at the terminals of the latter has reached a predetermined value, an air-gap is bridged, permitting the accumulated energy to be discharged through a circuit under resonant conditions, this resulting in a long series of isochronous impulses. These are either directly used or converted to any desired volume or pressure by means of a second circuit inductively linked with the first and tuned to the same. The facing diagram is taken from Tesla's lecture before the Franklin Institute and National Electric Light Association in 1893 and shows more elaborate arrangements of circuits, now quite familiar, for the conversion of ordinary direct or alternating currents into high frequency oscillations by this general method. In the mechanical apparatus illustrated, an attempt is made to convey an idea of the electrical operations as closely as practicable. The reciprocating and centrifugal pumps, respectively, represent an alternating and a direct current generator. The water takes the place of the electric fluid. The cylinder with its elastically restrained piston represents the condenser. The inertia of the moving parts corresponds to the self-induction of the electric circuit and the wide ports around the cylinder, through which the fluid can escape, perform the function of the air-gap. The operation of this apparatus will now be readily understood. Suppose first that the water is admitted to the cylinder from the centrifugal pump, this corresponding to the action of a continuous current generator. As the fluid is forced into the cylinder, the piston moves upward until the ports are uncovered, when a great quantity of the fluid rushes out, suddenly reducing the pressure so that the force of the compressed spring asserts itself and sends the piston down, closing the ports, whereupon these operations are repeated in as rapid succession as it may be desired. Each time the system, comprising the piston, rod, weights and adjustable spring, receives a blow, it quivers at its own rate which is determined by the inertia of the moving parts and the pliability of the spring exactly as in the electrical system the period of the circuit is determined by the self-induction and capacity. If, instead of the centrifugal, the reciprocating pump is employed, the operation is the same in principle except that the periodic impulses of the pump impose certain limitations. The greatest energy of movement will be obtained when synchronism is maintained between the pump impulses and the natural oscillations of the system.

Nikola Tesla and his famous wireless electric light. The gas-filled, phosphor-coated bulb anticipated in many respects the development, decades later, of fluorescent lighting.

V. THE MAGNIFYING
TRANSMITTER

AS I review the events of my past life I realize how subtle are the influences that shape our destinies. An incident of my youth may serve to illustrate. One winter's day I managed to climb a steep mountain, in company with other boys. The snow was quite deep and a warm southerly wind made it just suitable for our purpose. We amused ourselves by throwing balls which would roll down a certain distance, gathering more or less snow, and we tried to outdo one another in this exciting sport. Suddenly a ball was seen to go beyond the limit, swelling to enormous proportions until it became as big as a house and plunged thundering into the valley below with a force that made the ground tremble. I looked on spellbound, incapable of understanding what had happened. For weeks afterward the picture of the avalanche was before my eyes and I wondered how anything so small could grow to such an immense size. Ever since that time the magnification of feeble actions fascinated me, and when, years later, I took up the experimental study of mechanical and electrical resonance, I was keenly interested from the very start. Possibly, had it not been for that early powerful impression, I might not have followed up the little spark I obtained with my coil and never developed my best invention, the true history of which I will tell here for the first time.

"Lionhunters" have often asked me which of my discoveries I prize most. This depends on the point of view. Not a few technical men, very able in their special departments, but dominated by a pedantic spirit and nearsighted, have asserted that excepting the induction motor I have given to the world little of practical use. This is a grievous mistake. A new idea must not be judged by its immediate results. My alternating system of power transmission came at a psychological moment, as a long-sought answer to pressing industrial questions, and altho considerable resistance had to be overcome and opposing interests reconciled, as usual, the commercial introduction could not be long delayed. Now, compare this situation with that confronting my turbine, for example. One should think that so simple and beautiful an invention, possessing many features of an ideal motor, should be adopted at once and, undoubtedly, it would under similar conditions. But the prospective effect of the rotating field was not to render worthless existing machinery; on the contrary, it was to give it additional value. The system lent itself to new enterprise as well as to improvement of the old. My turbine is an advance of a character entirely different. It is a radical departure in the sense that its success would mean the abandonment of the antiquated types of prime movers on which billions of dollars have been spent. Under such circumstances the progress must needs be slow and perhaps the greatest impediment is encountered in the prejudicial opinions created in the minds of experts by organized opposition. Only the other day I had a disheartening experience when I met my friend and former assistant, Charles F. Scott, now professor of Electrical Engineering at Yale. I had not seen him for a long time and was glad to have an opportunity for a little chat at my office. Our conversation naturally enough drifted on my turbine and I became heated to a high degree. "Scott," I exclaimed, carried away by the vision of a glorious future, "my turbine will scrap all the heat-engines in the world." Scott stroked his chin and looked away thoughtfully, as though making a mental calculation. "That will make quite a pile of scrap," he said, and left without another word!

These and other inventions of mine, however, were nothing more than steps forward in certain directions. In evolving them I simply followed the inborn instinct to improve the present devices without any special thought of our far more imperative necessities. The "Magnifying Transmitter" was the product of labors extending through years, having for their chief object the solution of problems which are infinitely more important to mankind than mere industrial development.

If my memory serves me right, it was in November, 1890, that I performed a laboratory experiment which was one of

Tesla's bladeless turbine. Within the central, pancake-shaped housing are several discs, like flat, very-closely-spaced cultivator discs, which are fixed to the driveshaft seen projecting on either side. When air, steam, or another gas is injected under pressure between the discs, surface adhesion smoothly transfers the kinetic energy of the gas to the discs, causing rotation. Operated in reverse, the device can function as a gas compressor. (Tesla Museum/Smithsonian Institution)

the most extraordinary and spectacular ever recorded in the
annals of science. In investigating the behaviour of high
frequency currents I had satisfied myself that an electric field
of sufficient intensity could be produced in a room to light up
electrodeless vacuum tubes. Accordingly, a transformer was
built to test the theory and the first trial proved a marvelous
success. It is difficult to appreciate what those strange phenomena meant at that time. We crave for new sensations but
soon become indifferent to them. The wonders of yesterday
are today common occurrences. When my tubes were first
publicly exhibited they were viewed with amazement impossible to describe. From all parts of the world I received urgent
invitations and numerous honors and other flattering induce-
ments were offered to me, which I declined.

But in 1892 the demands became irresistible and I went to
London where I delivered a lecture before the Institution of
Electrical Engineers. It had been my intention to leave immediately for Paris in compliance with a similar obligation, but
Sir James Dewar insisted on my appearing before the Royal
Institution. I was a man of firm resolve but succumbed easily
to the forceful arguments of the great Scotchman. He pushed
me into a chair and poured out half a glass of a wonderful
brown fluid which sparkled in all sorts of iridescent colors
and tasted like nectar. "Now," said he, "you are sitting in
Faraday's chair and you are enjoying whiskey he used to
drink." In both aspects it was an enviable experience. The
next evening I gave a demonstration before that Institution, at
the termination of which Lord Rayleigh addressed the
audience and his generous words gave me the first start in
these endeavors. I fled from London and later from Paris to
escape favors showered upon me, and journeyed to my home
where I passed through a most painful ordeal and illness.
Upon regaining my health I began to formulate plans for the
resumption of work in America. Up to that time I never
realized that I possessed any particular gift of discovery but
Lord Rayleigh, whom I always considered as an ideal man of
science, had said so and if that was the case I felt that I should
concentrate on some big idea.

One day, as I was roaming in the mountains, I sought shelter from an approaching storm. The sky became overhung with heavy clouds but somehow the rain was delayed until, all of a sudden, there was a lightning flash and a few moments after a deluge. This observation set me thinking. It was manifest that the two phenomena were closely related, as cause and effect, and a little reflection led me to the conclusion that the electrical energy involved in the precipitation of the water was inconsiderable, the function of lightning being much like that of a sensitive trigger. Here was a stupendous possibility of achievement. If we could produce electric effects of the required quality, this whole planet and the conditions of existence on it could be transformed. The sun raises the water of the oceans and winds drive it to distant regions where it remains in a state of most delicate balance. If it were in our power to upset it when and wherever desired, this mighty life-sustaining stream could be at will controlled. We could irrigate arid deserts, create lakes and rivers and provide motive power in unlimited amounts. This would be the most efficient way of harnessing the sun to the uses of man. The consummation depended on our ability to develop electric forces of the order of those in nature. It seemed a hopeless undertaking, but I made up my mind to try it and immediately on my return to the United States, in the summer of 1892, work was begun which was to me all the more attractive, because a means of the same kind was necessary for the successful transmission of energy without wires.

The first gratifying result was obtained in the spring of the succeeding year when I reached tensions of about 1,000,000 volts with my conical coil. That was not much in the light of the present art, but it was then considered a feat. Steady progress was made until the destruction of my laboratory by fire in 1895, as may be judged from an article by T. C. Martin which appeared in the April number of the *Century Magazine*. This calamity set me back in many ways and most of that year had to be devoted to planning and reconstruction. However, as soon as circumstances permitted, I returned to the task. Although I knew that higher electro-motive forces were attain-

Tesla's gigantic wireless transmitter tower, erected in 1901-1903 at Shoreham, Long Island as part of his never-completed "World Wireless System." The huge scale of the 187-foot tower (which was demolished in 1917) may be judged from the two-story power plant seen in the background.

able with apparatus of larger dimensions, I had an instinctive perception that the object could be accomplished by the proper design of a comparatively small and compact transformer. In carrying on tests with a *secondary in the form of a flat spiral*, as illustrated in my patents, the absence of streamers surprised me, and it was not long before I discovered that this was due to the position of the turns and their mutual action. Profiting from this observation I resorted to the use of a high tension conductor with turns of considerable diameter sufficiently separated to keep down the distributed capacity, while at the same time preventing undue accumulation of the charge at any point. The application of this principle enabled me to produce pressures of 4,000,000 volts, which was about the limit obtainable in my new laboratory at Houston Street, as the discharges extended through a distance of 16 feet. A photograph of this transmitter was published in the *Electrical Review* of November, 1898. In order to advance further along this line I had to go into the open, and in the spring of 1899, having completed preparations for the erection of a wireless plant, I went to Colorado where I remained for more than one year. Here I introduced other improvements and refinements which made it possible to generate currents of any tension that may be desired. Those who are interested will find some information in regard to the experiments I conducted there in my article, "The Problem of Increasing Human Energy" in the *Century Magazine* of June, 1900, to which I have referred on a previous occasion.

I have been asked by the ELECTRICAL EXPERIMENTER to be quite explicit on this subject so that my young friends among the readers of the magazine will clearly understand the construction and operation of my "Magnifying Transmitter" and the purposes for which it is intended. Well, then, in the first place, it is a *resonant transformer* with a secondary in which the parts, charged to a high potential, are of considerable area and arranged in space along ideal enveloping surfaces of very large radii of curvature, and at proper distances from one another thereby insuring a *small electric surface density everywhere* so that *no leak can occur even if the conductor is bare.* It is suitable for any frequency, from a few to many thousands of cycles per second, and can be used in the production of currents of tremendous volume and moderate pressure, or of smaller amperage and immense electro-motive force. The maximum electric *tension is merely dependent on the curvature of the surfaces* on which the charged elements are situated and the area of the latter.

Judging from my past experience, as much as 100,000,000 volts are perfectly practicable. On the other hand currents of many thousands of amperes may be obtained in the antenna. A plant of but very moderate dimensions is required for such performances. Theoretically, a terminal of less than 90 feet in diameter is sufficient to develop an electro-motive force of that magnitude while for antenna currents of from 2,000-4,000 amperes at the usual frequencies it need not be larger than 30 feet in diameter.

In a more restricted meaning this wireless transmitter is one in which the Hertz-wave radiation is an entirely negligible quantity as compared with the whole energy, under which condition the damping factor is extremely small and an enormous charge is stored in the elevated capacity. Such a circuit may then be excited with impulses of any kind, even of low frequency and it will yield sinusoidal and continuous oscillations like those of an alternator.

Taken in the narrowest significance of the term, however, it is a resonant transformer which, besides possessing these qualities, is accurately proportioned to fit the globe and its electrical constants and properties, by virtue of which design it becomes highly efficient and effective in the wireless transmission of energy. Distance is then absolutely eliminated, there being *no diminution in the intensity of the transmitted impulses.* It is even possible to make the actions *increase with the distance from the plant* according to an exact mathematical law.

This invention was one of a number comprised in my "World-System" of wireless transmission which I undertook to commercialize on my return to New York in 1900. As to the immediate purposes of my enterprise, they were clearly outlined in a technical statement of that period from which I quote:

> "The 'World-System' has resulted from a combination of several original discoveries made by the inventor in the course of long continued research and experimentation. It makes possible not only the instantaneous and precise wireless transmission of any kind of signals, messages or characters, to all parts of the world, but also the inter-connection of the existing telegraph, telephone, and other signal stations without any change in their present equipment. By its means, for instance, a telephone subscriber here may call up and talk to any other subscriber on the Globe. An inexpensive receiver, not bigger than a watch, will enable him to listen anywhere, on land or sea, to a speech delivered or music played in some other place, however distant. These examples are cited merely to give an idea of the possibilities of this great scientific advance, which annihilates distance and makes that perfect natural conductor, the Earth, available for all the innumerable purposes which human ingenuity has found for a line-wire. One far-reaching result of this is that any device capable of being operated thru one or more wires (at a distance obviously restricted) can likewise be actuated, without artificial conductors and with the same facility and accuracy, at distances to which there are no limits other than those imposed by the physical dimensions of the Globe. Thus, not only will entirely new fields for commercial exploitation be opened up by this ideal method of transmission but the old ones vastly extended.

> "The 'World-System' is based on the application of the following important inventions and discoveries:

> "1. *The 'Tesla Transformer.'* This apparatus is in the production of electrical vibrations as revolutionary as gunpowder was in warfare. Currents many times stronger than any ever generated in the usual ways, and sparks over one hundred feet long, have been produced by the inventor with an instrument of this kind.

> "2. *The 'Magnifying Transmitter.'* This is Tesla's best invention—a peculiar transformer specially adapted to excite the Earth, which is in the transmission of electrical energy what the telescope is in astronomical observation. By the use of this marvelous device he has already set up electrical movements of greater intensity than those of lightning

and passed a current, sufficient to light more than two hundred incandescent lamps, around the Globe.

"3. *The 'Tesla Wireless System.'* This system comprises a number of improvements and is the only means known for transmitting economically electrical energy to a distance without wires. Careful tests and measurements in connection with an experimental station of great activity, erected by the inventor in Colorado, have demonstrated that power in any desired amount can be conveyed, clear across the Globe if necessary, with a loss not exceeding a few per cent.

"4. *The 'Art of Individualization.'* This invention of Tesla is to primitive 'tuning' what refined language is to unarticulated expression. It makes possible the transmission of signals or messages absolutely secret and exclusive both in the active and passive aspect, that is, non-interfering as well as non-interferable. Each signal is like an individual of unmistakable identity and there is virtually no limit to the number of stations or instruments which can be simultaneously operated without the slightest mutual disturbance.

"5. *'The terrestial Stationary Waves.'* This wonderful discovery, popularly explained, means that the Earth is responsive to electrical vibrations of definite pitch just as a tuning fork to certain waves of sound. These particular electrical vibrations, capable of powerfully exciting the Globe, lend themselves to innumerable uses of great importance commercially and in many other respects.

"The first 'World-System' power plant can be put in operation in nine months. With this power plant it will be practicable to attain electrical activities up to ten million horsepower and it is designed to serve for as many technical achievements as are possible without due expense. Among these the following may be mentioned:

"(1)   The inter-connection of the existing telegraph exchanges or offices all over the world;

"(2)   The establishment of a secret and non-interferable government telegraph service;

"(3)   The inter-connection of all the present telephone exchanges or offices on the Globe;

"(4)   The universal distribution of general news, by

Artist Frank Paul's conception of how the completed Long Island tower might have looked.

telegraph or telephone, in connection with the Press;

"(5)   The establishment of such a 'World-System' of intelligence transmission for exclusive private use;

"(6)   The inter-connection and operation of all stock tickers of the world;

"(7)   The establishment of a 'World-System' of musical distribution, etc.;

"(8)   The universal registration of time by cheap clocks indicating the hour with astronomical precision and requiring no attention whatever;

"(9)   The world transmission of typed or handwritten characters, letters, checks, etc.;

"(10)   The establishment of a universal marine service enabling the navigators of all ships to steer perfectly without compass, to determine the exact location, hour and speed, to prevent collisions and disasters, etc.;

"(11)   The inauguration of a system of world-printing on land and sea;

"(12)   The world reproduction of photographic pictures and all kinds of drawings or records."

I also proposed to make demonstrations in the wireless transmission of power on a small scale but sufficient to carry conviction. Besides these I referred to other and incomparably more important applications of my discoveries which will be disclosed at some future date.

A plant was built on Long Island with a tower 187 feet high, having a spherical terminal about 68 feet in diameter. These dimensions were adequate for the transmission of virtually any amount of energy. Originally only from 200 to 300 K.W. were provided but I intended to employ later several thousand horsepower. The transmitter was to emit a wave-complex of special characteristics and I had devised a unique method of telephonic control of any amount of energy.

The tower was destroyed two years ago but my projects are being developed and another one, improved in some features, will be constructed. On this occasion I would contradict the widely circulated report that the structure was demolished by the Government which owing to war conditions, might have created prejudice in the minds of those who may not know that the papers, which thirty years ago conferred upon me the honor of American citizenship, are always kept in a safe, while my orders, diplomas, degrees, gold medals and other distinctions are packed away in old trunks. If this report had a foundation I would have been refunded a large sum of money which I expended in the construction of the tower. On the contrary it was in the interest of the Government to preserve it, particularly as it would have made possible—to mention just one valuable result—the location of a submarine in any part of the world. My plant, services, and all my improvements have always been at the disposal of the officials and ever since the outbreak of the European conflict I have been working at a sacrifice on several inventions of mine relating to aerial navigation, ship propulsion and wireless transmission which are of the greatest importance to the country. Those who are well informed know that my ideas have revolutionized the industries of the United States and I am not aware that there lives an inventor who has been, in this respect, as fortunate as myself especially as regards the use of his improvements in the war. I have refrained from publicly expressing myself on this subject before as it seemed improper to dwell on personal matters while all the world was in dire trouble. I would add further, in view of various rumors which have reached me, that Mr. J. Pierpont Morgan did not interest himself with me in a business way but in the same large spirit in which he has assisted many other pioneers. He carried out his generous promise to the letter and it would have been most unreasonable to expect from him anything more. He had the highest regard for my attainments and gave me every evidence of his complete faith in my ability to ultimately achieve what I had set out to do. I am unwilling to accord to some small-minded and jealous individuals the satisfaction of having thwarted my efforts. These men are to me nothing more than microbes of a nasty disease. My project was retarded by laws of nature. The world was not prepared for it. It was too far ahead of time. But the same laws will prevail in the end and make it a triumphal success.

Nikola Tesla, aged 60, in a photograph taken the year he was awarded the Edison Medal by the American Institute of Electrical Engineers.

VI.   THE ART OF TELAUTOMATICS

No subject to which I have ever devoted myself has called for such concentration of mind and strained to so dangerous a degree the finest fibers of my brain as the system of which the Magnifying Transmitter is the foundation. I put all the intensity and vigor of youth in the development of the rotating field discoveries, but those early labors were of a different character. Although strenuous in the extreme, they did not involve that keen and exhausting discernment which had to be exercised in attacking the many puzzling problems of the wireless. Despite my rare physical endurance at that period the abused nerves finally rebelled and I suffered a complete collapse, just as the consummation of the long and difficult task was almost in sight. Without doubt I would have paid a greater penalty later, and very likely my career would have been prematurely terminated, had not providence equipt me with a safety device, which has seemed to improve with advancing years and unfailingly comes into play when my forces are at an end. So long as it operates I am safe from danger, due to overwork, which threatens other inventors and, incidentally, I need no vacations which are indispensable to most people. When I am all but used up I simply do as the darkies, who "naturally fall asleep while white folks worry." To venture a theory out of my sphere —the body probably accumulates little by little a definite quantity of some toxic agent and I sink into a nearly lethargic state which lasts half an hour to the minute. Upon awakening

I have the sensation as though the events immediately preceding had occurred very long ago, and if I attempt to continue the interrupted train of thought I feel a veritable mental nausea. Involuntarily I then turn to other work and am surprised at the freshness of the mind and ease with which I overcome obstacles that had baffled me before. After weeks or months my passion for the temporarily abandoned invention returns and I invariably find answers to all the vexing questions with scarcely any effort. In this connection I will tell of an extraordinary experience which may be of interest to students of psychology. I had produced a striking phenomenon with my grounded transmitter and was endeavoring to ascertain its true significance in relation to the currents propagated through the earth. It seemed a hopeless undertaking, and for more than a year I worked unremittingly, but in vain. This profound study so entirely absorbed me that I became forgetful of everything else, even of my undermined health. At last, as I was at the point of breaking down, nature applied the preservative inducing lethal sleep. Regaining my senses, I realized with consternation that I was unable to visualize scenes from my life except those of infancy, the very first ones that had entered my consciousness. Curiously enough, these appeared before my vision with startling distinctness and afforded me welcome relief. Night after night, when retiring, I would think of them and more and more of my previous existence was revealed. The image of my mother was always the principal figure in the spectacle that slowly unfolded, and a consuming desire to see her again gradually took possession of me. This feeling grew so strong that I resolved to drop all work and satisfy my longing. But I found it too hard to break away from the laboratory, and several months elapsed during which I had succeeded in reviving all the impressions of my past life up to the spring of 1892. In the next picture that came out of the mist of oblivion, I saw myself at the *Hotel de la Paix* in Paris just coming to from one of my peculiar sleeping spells, which had been caused by prolonged exertion of the brain. Imagine the pain and distress I felt when it flashed upon my mind that a dispatch was handed to me at that very moment bearing the sad news that my mother was dying. I remembered how I made the long journey home without an hour of rest and how she passed away after weeks of agony! It was especially remarkable that during all this period of partially obliterated memory I was fully alive to everything touching on the subject of my research. I could recall the smallest details and the least significant observations in my experiments and even recite pages of text and complex mathematical formulae.

My belief is firm in a law of compensation. The true rewards are ever in proportion to the labor and sacrifices made. This is one of the reasons why I feel certain that of all my inventions, the Magnifying Transmitter will prove most important and valuable to future generations. I am prompted to this prediction not so much by thoughts of the commercial and industrial revolution which it will surely bring about, but of the humanitarian consequences of the many achievements it makes possible. Considerations of mere utility weigh little in the balance against the higher benefits of civilization. We are confronted with portentous problems which can not be solved just by providing for our material existence, however abundantly. On the contrary, progress in this direction is fraught with hazards and perils not less menacing than those born from want and suffering. If we were to release the energy of atoms or discover some other way of developing cheap and unlimited power at any point of the globe this accomplishment, instead of being a blessing, might bring disaster to mankind in giving rise to dissension and anarchy which would ultimately result in the enthronement of the hated regime of force. The greatest good will come from technical improvements tending to unification and harmony, and my wireless transmitter is preeminently such. By its means the human voice and likeness will be reproduced everywhere and factories driven thousands of miles from waterfalls furnishing the power; aerial machines will be propelled around the earth without a stop and the sun's energy controlled to create lakes and rivers for motive purposes and transformation of arid deserts into fertile land. Its introduction for telegraphic, telephonic and similar uses will automatically cut out the statics and all other interferences which at present impose narrow limits to the application of the wireless. This is a timely topic on which a few words might not be amiss.

During the past decade a number of people have arrogantly claimed that they had succeeded in doing away with this impediment. I have carefully examined all of the arrangements described and tested most of them long before they were publicly disclosed, but the finding was uniformly negative. A recent official statement from the U.S. Navy may, perhaps, have taught some beguilable news editors how to appraise these announcments at their real worth. As a rule the attempts are based on theories so fallacious that whenever they come to my notice I can not help thinking in a lighter vein. Quite recently a new discovery was heralded, with a deafening flourish of trumpets, but it proved another case of a mountain bringing forth a mouse. This reminds me of an exciting incident which took place years ago when I was conducting my experiments with currents of high frequency. Steve Brodie had just jumped off the Brooklyn Bridge. The feat has been vulgarized since by imitators, but the first report electrified New York. I was very impressionable then and frequently spoke of the daring printer. On a hot afternoon I felt the necessity of refreshing myself and stepped into one of the popular thirty thousand institutions of this great city where a delicious twelve per cent beverage was served which can now be had only by making a trip to the poor and devastated countries of Europe. The attendance was large and not over-distinguished and a matter was discussed which gave me an admirable opening for the careless remark: "This is what I said when I jumped off the bridge." No sooner had I uttered these words than I felt like the companion of Timotheus in the poem of Schiller. In an instant there was a pandemonium and a dozen voices cried: "It is Brodie!" I threw a quarter on the counter and bolted for the door but the crowd was at my heels with yells: "Stop, Steve!" which must have been misunderstood for many persons tried to hold me up as I ran frantically for my haven of refuge. By darting around corners I fortunately managed — through the medium of a fire-escape — to reach the laboratory where I threw off my coat, camouflaged myself as a hard-working blacksmith, and started the forge.

But these precautions proved unnecessary; I had eluded my pursuers. For many years afterward, at night, when imagination turns into spectres the trifling troubles of the day, I often thought, as I tossed on the bed, what my fate would have been had that mob caught me and found out that I was not Steve Brodie!

Now the engineer, who lately gave an account before a technical body of a novel remedy against statics based on a "heretofore unknown law of nature," seems to have been as reckless as myself when he contended that these disturbances propagate up and down, while those of a transmitter proceed along the earth. It would mean that a condenser, as this globe, with its gaseous envelope, could be charged and discharged in a manner quite contrary to the fundamental teachings propounded in every elemental text-book of physics. Such a supposition would have been condemned as erroneous, even in Franklin's time, for the facts bearing on this were then well known and the identity between atmospheric electricity and that developed by machines was fully established. Obviously, natural and artificial disturbances propagate through the earth and the air in exactly the same way, and both set up electro-motive forces in the horizontal, as well as vertical, sense. Interference can not be overcome by any such methods as were proposed. The truth is this. In the air the potential increases at the rate of about fifty volts per foot of elevation, owing to which there may be a difference of pressure amounting to twenty, or even forty thousand volts between the upper and lower ends of the antenna. The masses of the charged atmosphere are constantly in motion and give up electricity to the conductor, not continuously but rather disruptively, this producing a grinding noise in a sensitive telephonic receiver. The higher the terminal and the greater the space encompast by the wires, the more pronounced is the effect, but it must be understood that it is purely local and has little to do with the real trouble. In 1900, while perfecting my wireless system, one form of apparatus comprised four antennae. These were carefully calibrated to the same frequency and connected in multiple with the object of magnifying the action, in receiving from any direction. When I desired to ascertain the origin of the transmitted impulses, each diagonally situated pair was put in series with a primary coil energizing the detector circuit. In the former case the sound was loud in the telephone; in the latter it ceased, as expected, the two antennae neutralizing each other, but the true statics manifested themselves in both instances and I had to devise special preventives embodying different principles.

By employing receivers connected to two points of the ground, as suggested by me long ago, this trouble caused by the charged air, which is very serious in the structures as now built, is nullified and besides, the liability of all kinds of interference is reduced to about one-half, because of the directional character of the circuit. This was perfectly self-evident, but came as a revelation to some simple-minded wireless folks whose experience was confined to forms of apparatus that could have been improved with an axe, and they have been disposing of the bear's skin before killing him. If it were true that strays performed such antics, it would be easy to get rid of them by receiving without aerials. But, as a matter of fact, a wire buried in the ground which, conforming to this view, should be absolutely immune, is more susceptible to certain extraneous impulses than one placed vertically in the air. To state it fairly, a slight progress has been made, but not by virtue of any particular method or device. It was achieved simply by discarding the enormous structures, which are bad enough for transmission but wholly unsuitable for reception, and adopting a more appropriate type of receiver. As I pointed out in a previous article, to dispose of this difficulty for good, a radical change must be made in the system, and the sooner this is done the better.

It would be calamitous, indeed, if at this time when the art is in its infancy and the vast majority, not excepting even experts, have no conception of its ultimate possibilities, a measure would be rushed through the legislature making it a government monopoly. This was proposed a few weeks ago by Secretary Daniels, and no doubt that distinguished official has made his appeal to the Senate and House of Representatives with sincere conviction. But universal evidence unmistakably shows that the best results are always obtained in healthful commercial competition. There are, however, exceptional reasons why wireless should be given the fullest freedom of development. In the first place it offers prospects immeasurably greater and more vital to betterment of human life than any other invention or discovery in the history of man. Then again, it must be understood that this wonderful art has been, in its entirety, evolved here and can be called "American" with more right and propriety than the telephone, the incandescent lamp or the aeroplane. Enterprising press agents and stock jobbers have been so successful in spreading misinformation that even so excellent a periodical as the *Scientific American* accords the chief credit to a foreign country. The Germans, of course, gave us the Hertz-waves and the Russian, English, French and Italian experts were quick in using them for signaling purposes. It was an obvious application of the new agent and accomplished with the old classical and unimproved induction coil — scarcely anything more than another kind of heliography. The radius of transmission was very limited, the results attained of little value, and the Hertz oscillations, as a means for conveying intelligence, could have been advantageously replaced by sound-waves, which I advocated in 1891. Moreover, all of these attempts were made three years after the basic principles of the wireless system, which is universally employed to-day, and its potent instrumentalities had been clearly described and developed in America. No trace of those Hertzian appliances and methods remains today. We have proceeded in the very opposite direction and what has been done is the product of the brains and efforts of citizens of this country. The fundamental patents have expired and the opportunities are open to all. The chief argument of the Secretary is based on interference. According to his statement, reported in the New York *Herald* of July 29th, signals from a powerful station can be intercepted in every village of the world. In view of this fact, which was demonstrated in my experiments of 1900, it would be of little use to impose restrictions in the United States.

As throwing light on this point, I may mention that only recently an odd looking gentleman called on me with the object of enlisting my services in the construction of world transmitters in some distant land. "We have no money," he said, "but carloads of solid gold and we will give you a liberal amount." I told him that I wanted to see first what will be done with my inventions in America, and this ended the interview. But I am satisfied that some dark forces are at work, and as time goes on the maintenance of continuous communication will be rendered more difficult. The only remedy is a system immune against interruption. It has been perfected, it exists, and all that is necessary is to put it in operation.

The terrible conflict is still uppermost in the minds and perhaps the greatest importance will be attached to the Magnifying Transmitter as a machine for attack and defense, more particularly in connection with *Telautomatics*. This invention is a logical outcome of observations begun in my boyhood and continued thruout my life. When the first results were publisht the *Electrical Review* stated editorially that it would become one of the "most potent factors in the advance and civilization of mankind." The time is not distant when this prediction will be fulfilled. In 1898 and 1900 it was offered to the Government and might have been adopted were I one of those who would go to Alexander's shepherd when they want a favor from Alexander. At that time I really thought that it would abolish war, because of its unlimited destructiveness and exclusion of the personal element of combat. But while I

One of Tesla's wirelessly-controlled boats, submersible and without external aerials.

have not lost faith in its potentialities, my views have changed since.

War can not be avoided until the physical cause for its recurrence is removed and this, in the last analysis, is the vast extent of the planet on which we live. Only thru annihilation of distance in every respect, as the conveyance of intelligence, transport of passengers and supplies and transmission of energy will conditions be brought about some day, insuring permanency of friendly relations. What we now want most is closer contact and better understanding between individuals and communities all over the earth, and the elimination of that fanatic devotion to exalted ideals of national egoism and pride which is always prone to plunge the world into primeval barbarism and strife. No league or parliamentary act of any kind will ever prevent such a calamity. These are only new devices for putting the weak at the mercy of the strong. I have exprest myself in this regard fourteen years ago, when a combination of a few leading governments — a sort of Holy Alliance — was advocated by the late Andrew Carnegie, who may be fairly considered as the father of this idea, having given to it more publicity and impetus than anybody else prior to the efforts of the President. While it can not be denied that such a pact might be of material advantage to some less fortunate peoples, it can not attain the chief object sought. Peace can only come as a natural consequence of universal enlightenment and merging of races, and we are still far from this blissful realization. As I view the world of today, in the light of the gigantic struggle we have witnest, I am filled with conviction that the interests of humanity would be best served if the United States remained true to its traditions and kept out of "entangling alliances." Situated as it is, geographically, remote from the theaters of impending conflicts, without incentive to territorial aggrandizement, with inexhaustible resources and immense population thoroly imbued with the spirit of liberty and right, this country is placed in a unique and privileged position. It is thus able to exert, independently, its colossal strength and moral force to the benefit of all, more judiciously and effectively, than as member of a league.

In one of these biographical sketches, published in the

ELECTRICAL EXPERIMENTER, I have dwelt on the circumstances of my early life and told of an affliction which compelled me to unremitting exercise of imagination and self-
observation. This mental activity, at first involuntary under
the pressure of illness and suffering, gradually became second
nature and led me finally to recognize that I was but an
automaton devoid of free will in thought and action and
merely responsive to the forces of the environment. Our bodies
are of such complexity of structure, the motions we perform
are so numerous and involved, and the external impressions
on our sense organs to such a degree delicate and elusive that it
is hard for the average person to grasp this fact. And yet
nothing is more convincing to the trained investigator than
the mechanistic theory of life which had been, in a measure,
understood and propounded by Descartes three hundred years
ago. But in his time many important functions of our organism were unknown and, especially with respect to the nature
of light and the construction and operation of the eye, phi-
losophers were in the dark. In recent years the progress of
scientific research in these fields has been such as to leave no
room for a doubt in regard to this view on which many works
have been published. One of its ablest and most eloquent
exponents is, perhaps, Felix Le Dantec, formerly assistant of
Pasteur. Prof. Jacques Loeb has performed remarkable experiments in heliotropism, clearly establishing the controlling
power of light in lower forms of organisms, and his latest
book, "Forced Movements," is revelatory. But while men of
science accept this theory simply as any other that is recognized, to me it is a truth which I hourly demonstrate by every
act and thought of mine. The consciousness of the external
impression prompting me to any kind of exertion, physical or
mental, is ever present in my mind. Only on very rare occasions, when I was in a state of exceptional concentration, have
I found difficulty in locating the original impulses.

The by far greater number of human beings are never
aware of what is passing around and within them, and millions fall victims of disease and die prematurely just on this
account. The commonest, every-day occurrences appear to

them mysterious and inexplicable. One may feel a sudden wave of sadness and rake his brain for an explanation when he might have noticed that it was caused by a cloud cutting off the rays of the sun. He may see the image of a friend dear to him under conditions which he construes as very peculiar, when only shortly before he has passed him in the street or seen his photograph somewhere. When he loses a collar button he fusses and swears for an hour, being unable to visualize his previous actions and locate the object directly. Deficient observation is merely a form of ignorance and responsible for the many morbid notions and foolish ideas prevailing. There is not more than one out of every ten persons who does not believe in telepathy and other psychic manifestations, spiritualism and communion with the dead, and who would refuse to listen to willing or unwilling deceivers. Just to illustrate how deeply rooted this tendency has become even among the clear-headed American population, I may mention a comical incident.

Shortly before the war, when the exhibition of my turbines in this city elicited widespread comment in the technical papers, I anticipated that there would, be a scramble among manufacturers to get hold of the invention, and I had particular designs on that man from Detroit who has an uncanny faculty for accumulating millions. So confident was I that he would turn up some day, that I declared this as certain to my secretary and assistants. Sure enough, one fine morning a body of engineers from the Ford Motor Company presented themselves with the request of discussing with me an important project. "Didn't I tell you?" I remarked triumphantly to my employees, and one of them said, "You are amazing, Mr. Tesla; everything comes out exactly as you predict." As soon as these hard-headed men were seated I, of course, immediately began to extol the wonderful features of my turbine, when the spokesmen interrupted me and said, "We know all about this, but we are on a special errand. We have formed a psychological society for the investigation of psychic phenomena and we want you to join us in this undertaking." I suppose those engineers never knew how near they came to being fired out of my office.

Ever since I was told by some of the greatest men of the time, leaders in science whose names are immortal, that I am possesst of an unusual mind, I bent all my thinking faculties on the solution of great problems regardless of sacrifice. For many years I endeavored to solve the enigma of death, and watched eagerly for every kind of spiritual indication. But only once in the course of my existence have I had an experience which momentarily impressed me as supernatural. It was at the time of my mother's death. I had become completely exhausted by pain and long vigilance, and one night was carried to a building about two blocks from our home. As I lay helpless there, I thought that if my mother died while I was away from her bedside she would surely give me a sign. Two or three months before I was in London in company with my late friend, Sir William Crookes, when spiritualism was discussed, and I was under the full sway of these thoughts. I might not have paid attention to other men, but was susceptible to his arguments as it was his epochal work on radiant matter, which I had read as a student, that made me embrace the electrical career. I reflected that the conditions for a look into the beyond were most favorable, for my mother was a woman of genius and particularly excelling in the powers of intuition. During the whole night every fiber in my brain was strained in expectancy, but nothing happened until early in the morning, when I fell in a sleep, or perhaps a swoon, and saw a cloud carrying angelic figures of marvelous beauty, one of whom gazed upon me lovingly and gradually assumed the features of my mother. The appearance slowly floated across the room and vanished, and I was awakened by an indescribably sweet song of many voices. In that instant a certitude, which no words can express, came upon me that my mother had just died. And that was true. I was unable to understand the tremendous weight of the painful knowledge I received in advance, and wrote a letter to Sir William Crookes while still under the domination of these impressions and in poor bodily health. When I recovered I sought for a long time the external cause of this strange manifestation and, to my great relief, I succeeded after many months of fruitless effort. I had seen the painting of a celebrated artist, representing allegorically one of the seasons in the form of a cloud with a group of angels which seemed to actually float in the air, and this had struck me forcefully. It was exactly the same that appeared in my dream, with the exception of my mother's likeness. The music came from the choir in the church nearby at the early mass of Easter morning, explaining everything satisfactorily in conformity with scientific facts.

This occurred long ago, and I have never had the faintest reason since to change my views on psychical and spiritual phenomena, for which there is absolutely no foundation. The belief in these is the natural outgrowth of intellectual development. Religious dogmas are no longer accepted in their orthodox meaning, but every individual clings to faith in a supreme power of some kind. We all must have an ideal to govern our conduct and insure contentment, but it is immaterial whether it be one of creed, art, science or anything else, so long as it fulfills the function of a dematerializing force. It is essential to the peaceful existence of humanity as a whole that one common conception should prevail.

While I have failed to obtain any evidence in support of the contentions of psychologists and spiritualists, I have proved to my complete satisfaction the automatism of life, not only through continuous observations of individual actions, but even more conclusively through certain generalizations. These amount to a discovery which I consider of the greatest moment to human society, and on which I shall briefly dwell. I got the first inkling of this astounding truth when I was still a very young man, but for many years I interpreted what I noted simply as coincidences. Namely, whenever either myself or a person to whom I was attached, or a cause to which I was devoted, was hurt by others in a particular way, which might be best popularly characterized as the most unfair imaginable, I experienced a singular and undefinable pain which, for want of a better term, I have qualified as "cosmic," and shortly thereafter, and invariably, those who had inflicted it came to grief. After many such cases I confided this to a number of friends, who had the opportunity to convince themselves of the truth of the theory which I have gradually formulated and which may be stated in the following few words:

Our bodies are of similar construction and exposed to the same external influences. This results in likeness of response and concordance of the general activities on which all our social and other rules and laws are based. We are automata entirely controlled by the forces of the medium being tossed about like corks on the surface of the water, but mistaking the resultant of the impulses from the outside for free will. The movements and other actions we perform are always life preservative and tho seemingly quite independent from one another, we are connected by invisible links. So long as the organism is in perfect order it responds accurately to the agents that prompt it, but the moment that there is some derangement in any individual, his self-preservative power is impaired. Everybody understands, of course, that if one becomes deaf, has his eyesight weakened, or his limbs injured, the chances for his continued existence are lessened. But this is also true, and perhaps more so, of certain defects in the brain which deprive the automaton, more or less, of that vital quality and cause it to rush into destruction. A very sensitive and observant being, with his highly developed mechanism all intact, and acting with precision in obedience to the changing conditions of the environment, is endowed with a transcending mechanical sense, enabling him to evade perils too subtle to be directly perceived. When he comes in contact with others whose controlling organs are radically faulty, that sense asserts itself and he feels the "cosmic" pain. The truth of this has been borne out in hundreds of instances and I am inviting other students of nature to devote attention to this subject, believing that thru combined and systematic effort results of incalculable value to the world will be attained.

The idea of constructing an automaton, to bear out my theory, presented itself to me early but I did not begin active work until 1893, when I started my wireless investigations. During the succeeding two or three years a number of automatic mechanisms, to be actuated from a distance, were constructed by me and exhibited to visitors in my laboratory. In

1896, however, I designed a complete machine capable of a multitude of operations, but the consummation of my labors was delayed until late in 1897. This machine was illustrated and described in my article in the Century Magazine of June, 1900, and other periodicals of that time and, when first shown in the beginning of 1898, it created a sensation such as no other invention of mine has ever produced. In November, 1898, a basic patent on the novel art was granted to me, but only after the Examiner-in-Chief had come to New York and witnesst the performance, for what I claimed seemed unbelievable. I remember that when later I called on an official in Washington, with a view of offering the invention to the Government, he burst out in laughter upon my telling him what I had accomplished. Nobody thought then that there was the faintest prospect of perfecting such a device. It is unfortunate that in this patent, following the advice of my attorneys, I indicated the control as being effected thru the medium of a single circuit and a well-known form of detector, for the reason that I had not yet secured protection on my methods and apparatus for individualization. As a matter of fact, my boats were controlled thru the joint action of several circuits and interference of every kind was excluded. Most generally I employed receiving circuits in the form of loops, including condensers, because the discharges of my high-tension transmitter ionized the air in the hall so that even a very small aerial would draw electricity from the surrounding atmosphere for hours. Just to give an idea, I found, for instance, that a bulb 12″ in diameter, highly exhausted, and with one single terminal to which a short wire was attached, would deliver well on to one thousand successive flashes before all charge of the air in the laboratory was neutralized. The loop form of receiver was not sensitive to such a disturbance and it is curious to note that it is becoming popular at this late date. In reality it collects much less energy than the aerials or a long grounded wire, but it so happens that it does away with a number of defects inherent to the present wireless devices. In demonstrating my invention before audiences, the visitors were requested to ask any questions, however involved, and the automaton would answer

Artist Paul's conception of Tesla's self-propelled Telautomaton. Tesla described this as a missile driven entirely by reaction, capable of travelling at 350 miles per hour to land within a few feet of a target a thousand miles away.

them by signs. This was considered magic at that time but was extremely simple, for it was myself who gave the replies by means of the device.

At the same period another larger telautomatic boat was constructed, a photograph of which is shown in this number of the ELECTRICAL EXPERIMENTER. It was controlled by loops, having several turns placed in the hull, which was made entirely water-tight and capable of submergence. The apparatus was similar to that used in the first with the exception of certain special features I introduced as, for example, incandescent lamps which afforded a visible evidence of the proper functioning of the machine.

These automata, controlled within the range of vision of the operator, were, however, the first and rather crude steps in the evolution of the Art of Telautomatics as I had conceived it. The next logical improvement was its application to automatic mechanisms beyond the limits of vision and at great distance from the center of control, and I have ever since advocated their employment as instruments of warfare in preference to guns. The importance of this now seems to be recognized, if I am to judge from casual announcements thru the press of achievements which are said to be extraordinary but contain no merit of novelty, whatever. In an imperfect manner it is practicable, with the existing wireless plants, to launch an aeroplane, have it follow a certain approximate course, and perform some operation at a distance of many hundreds of miles. A machine of this kind can also be mechanically controlled in several ways and I have no doubt that it may prove of some usefulness in war. But there are, to my best knowledge, no instrumentalities in existence today with which such an object could be accomplished in a precise manner. I have devoted years of study to this matter and have evolved means, making such and greater wonders easily realizable. As stated on a previous occasion, when I was a student at college I conceived a flying machine quite unlike the present ones. The underlying principle was sound but could not be carried into practice for want of a prime-mover of sufficiently great activity. In recent years I have successfully solved this problem and am now planning aerial machines devoid of sustaining planes, ailerons, propellers and other external attachments, which will be capable of immense speeds and are very likely to furnish powerful arguments for peace in the near future. Such a machine, sustained and propelled entirely by reaction, is shown on page 108 and is supposed to be controlled either mechanically or by wireless energy. By installing proper plants it will be practicable to project a missile of this kind into the air and drop it almost on the very spot designated, which may be thousands of miles away. But we are not going to stop at this. Telautomata will be ultimately produced, capable of acting as if possesst of their own intelligence, and their advent will create a revolution. As early as 1898 I proposed to representatives of a large manufacturing concern the construction and public exhibition of an automobile carriage which, left to itself, would perform a great variety of operations involving something akin to judgment. But my proposal was deemed chimerical at that time and nothing came from it.

At present many of the ablest minds are trying to devise expedients for preventing a repetition of the awful conflict which is only theoretically ended and the duration and main issues of which I have correctly predicted in an article printed in the *Sun* of December 20, 1914. The proposed League is not a remedy but on the contrary, in the opinion of a number of competent men, may bring about results just the opposite. It is particularly regrettable that a punitive policy was adopted in framing the terms of peace, because a few years hence it will be possible for nations to fight without armies, ships or guns, by weapons far more terrible, to the destructive action and range of which there is virtually no limit. A city, at any distance whatsoever from the enemy, can be destroyed by him and no power on earth can stop him from doing so. If we want to avert an impending calamity and a state of things which may transform this globe into an inferno, we should push the development of flying machines and wireless transmission of energy without an instant's delay and with all the power and resources of the nation.

Appendix: *The original rendering and original caption of the Hydraulic Analog from Chapter III of My Inventions. If the reader has understood the operation of the polyphase rotating magnetic field, he or she will immediately see that the three parts of the diagram are **themselves** "out-of-phase."*

DATE DUE

8-18-10			
4-11-11			
3-20-15			
GAYLORD			PRINTED IN U.S.A.